The Tulip Tea
Twenty-Four Hours in NYC

Perrie Patterson

Copyright © 2023 Perrie Patterson

All rights reserved. No part of this publication may be reproduced, distributed, or transmitted in any form or by any means, including photocopying, recording, or other electronic or mechanical methods, without prior written permission of the publisher except in cases of brief quotations embodied in reviews and other noncommercial use permitted by copyright law. For permission requests, contact the author at
www.perripatterson.com

ISBN #979-8-8689-5469-6 IngramSpark for retailers.

The cover design is a collaboration by University of Alabama student Victoria Buckley (@v.a.buckley @Victoria.buckley_photography) and University of Georgia student and the author's daughter, Laine Tucker.

Dedicated to the incredible, talented, and award-winning author

Judy Blume

Had it not been for Judy Blume's books, I would have never found my insatiable interest in reading. It was the late 1970s when Judy Blume's middle-grade books hooked me from the start and kept me reading way into the dark. Thank you, Judy Blume, for creating books for kids, teens and adults that tell realistic life stories that to this day still inspire creativity, and a passion for reading. And guess what? I still have my original set of middle-grade Judy Blume books! Those books are well loved, and so are you, Judy!

1
Office Shenanigans

For Holly Curtis, the morning commute started off like a Monday, although it was Tuesday. She couldn't find her favorite travel coffee mug, so she grabbed what was clean, but she couldn't find a lid to fit and soon gave up looking.

She was out of her favorite oat milk; it seemed as if only a teaspoonful had landed in her drink. After tossing the carton into the trash, she quickly added a few drops of regular milk and a drop of heavy cream. Her roommate's orange cat, Padre, jumped up onto the counter, looking for any spills.

"Nothing for you here, boy," Holly said. After checking to make sure Padre still had food in his bowl, she gave him a head rub, then picked up her coffee.

Juggling her bag and mug while trying not to spill anything from the open container on herself while she walked to her car was a challenge. She admired the weather, smiling to herself, glad that as late March approached, signs of spring were everywhere. Finally, she pulled out of her parking spot.

Her heart pounded in her chest as a loud honk startled her almost into the next year. After the angry driver zoomed past, she caught her breath, and slapped her hand across the screen on her dash that obviously wasn't working.

"Is my backup camera picking the days when it wants to work and when it doesn't? Geez. What day is it again?" she asked herself.

She got cut off while trying to merge into a left-turn lane but refused to blow her horn at anyone. Holly hated horns and road-ragers, wishing people could go about driving without all the fuss and drama. Atlanta traffic was usually terrible, and some days it was hard enough to get to work on time. She could do without the trip to Camp Grinchmas. "Why are people so rude?" she said to herself.

Twenty minutes later, Holly was pulling into the parking lot for the magazine she'd worked for since graduating college. *Beyond*, the newest, trendiest Atlanta-based magazine, highlighted young, up-and-coming businesswomen, not only from Atlanta but from anywhere in the world. It had been the dream-child of its founder and editor in chief, Marla Monroe, who graduated three years ago from Cal Berkley with a degree in journalism and a minor in marketing.

The magazine still had only a skeleton staff. Even though it was getting rave reviews on everything from its blogs to its brand-new podcast, there just weren't enough funds yet to hire more than the current crew of six employees. Or that would be seven, if you counted Marla's boyfriend, Michael, who occasionally filled in in a pinch. Their hard-copy issues only came out twice a year, and Marla made sure those were epic with hard-hitting stories about women entrepreneurs, female athletes, and small-town heroes no one would ever hear about if not for *Beyond*.

For the fall issue, Marla had interviewed Sara Blakely, the Atlanta-based businesswoman who founded Spanx. Sara had started her shapewear business with five thousand dollars of her own money, a unique idea, and a killer determination and drive that launched her into the success lane. So far, that issue has been the most successful in sales and has brought more attention to the magazine. The downside of that is Marla refusing to take a break. And we're not talking just a quick lunch break; she hadn't had a significant vacation since she started *Beyond*.

You could say Holly was beyond grateful (pun intended) to work for *Beyond*. Landing a position as a writer and blogger for the magazine right out of college had been a dream. But Holly wanted more success and for the past year had many times mentioned to Marla she'd love an opportunity to write a cover story. She knew that writing a cover might launch her career as a real journalist, which could lead her to other opportunities. She just hoped one day Marla would trust her enough with the challenge, and that Marla could relax enough to relinquish control that would allow others to step up and shine.

Holly tossed her bag over one shoulder, and adjusted her silk, light-pink Golden Goose scarf, which was tied in a simple knot around her neck and paired quite nicely with her cream baby-doll-style dress. She paused to take a refreshing deep breath before making her way through the office doors. So far, so good; she'd made it to the office without so much as a spill. As she stepped through the doors, she checked her phone for the time. *Not late*, she thought, then took a sip of her drink.

"Coffee?"

The voice caused Holly to jump, and she'd just taken a sip. Creamy brown droplets dribbled from her open coffee container onto the front of her dress. She had not been expecting a door greeting or anybody proffering coffee. Her co-worker Wagner Stein, who runs the weekly podcast interviews and the website, greeted Holly with a happy "Good morning" while holding out a cup for her to take. He stood there with a pleasant smile gracing his clean-shaven face.

Holly shook her head, and a strand of loose, wavy blonde hair fell over her left eye. She tossed her head to the side and her bob-style locks fell back into place. "Thanks, but I brought some with me today."

Wagner appeared to be completely oblivious to the fact that he'd startled Holly with the quick greeting at the door, causing her to dribble coffee on herself. Quickly, she dug around in her bag looking for the package of Tide wipes she usually carried. Wagner moved into step beside her as she made her way to her desk.

"Uh, don't forget it's team trivia night at Hob Nob," Wagner said. "I'd be glad to give you a ride."

"Right. Thanks for the reminder, Wagner."

Holly pulled the wipes from her bag and began to walk a bit faster. But Wagner stuck next to her like a hair in the sink that refused to go down the drain.

"I mean," Wagner continued, "I know you drove here, but carpooling saves gas, the environment, the ecosystem, the ducks."

"Huh?" Holly said, turning to look directly at him.

Wagner had a goofy grin on his face. His frame was tall and thin. To Holly, it was obvious that he liked wearing khakis and button-down collared shirts, which gave him a smart, preppy appearance. He reminded her of someone who might be on a school debate team. Although Wagner's look was neat, Holly thought his curly brown hair could do with a quick comb-through, maybe even some product.

"You know, saving ducks from oil spills in the ocean," he replied.

Holly shook her head to clear the thought of baby ducks covered in oil, then she set her bag down next to her desk, placed her mug near the corner, pulled a Tide wipe from the package, and started vigorously wiping the spill, which by now had started to dry. Before she pulled out her chair, she turned to Wagner. "Yeah, okay, Wagner. I know. But I need to get to work now."

Stella, another writer, who sat next to Holly, leaned back in her chair and caught Holly's eye. Then Stella glanced at Wagner, who was standing nearby, almost like a puppy waiting for a treat or for someone to throw him a ball. His interest in having Holly's attention was so.... well, let's say, "fetching," even "adorable." He stuffed his hands into the front pockets of his khaki pants.

"Wagner," Stella said. "You know, Kali, Holly, and I usually ride to trivia together, but you are welcome to join us."

Wagner's eyes lit up. Holly glared at Stella, her eyes frozen and unblinking. She tried doing her best to send her a mental message of *Gurrrrl! Have you lost your ever-lovin' mind?*

Holly's eyes remained on Stella. "Remember, Marla was planning to go tonight," Holly said. "There might not be enough room in Kali's car." With that, she turned away, opened her laptop, and turned it on, just as her phone rang.

"Hello," Holly answered.

Wagner walked away. Stella chuckled. Holly squinted her cornflower-blue eyes at Stella then stood, as she listened to the caller.

"Yes, I'll be right there," Holly said before hanging up. "Marla needs me. She says it's urgent. I'll be back." She paused. A Cheshire-cat grin captured her features. "With a vengeance," she added with a teasing tone, then wiggled her fingers in a wave and tossed her used wipe onto Stella's desk.

Stella shook her head and called over her shoulder, "You know I'm not sure if you're quoting *Die Hard* or *The Terminator,*" she said, then went back to work, still chuckling about Holly's office admirer.

2

The Assignment

When Holly walked into Marla's office, her boss was on another phone call, so she stood near the entrance waiting, not wanting to intrude. As soon as Marla looked up and saw Holly, she motioned for her to sit in one of the two bright, floral-print chairs situated in front of Marla's desk.

"Perfect. Thanks, Gary. I owe you one," Marla said before ending the call.

While putting her phone away, Marla took a guzzle from a can of cotton-candy-flavored Bang then set it down on a chunky, white-marble coaster. She flung her long, straight dark hair over one shoulder, and a huge smile lit up her face before she stood up and walked around to the front of her desk. After leaning her skinny butt against the front edge, Marla kicked off her shiny patent-leather hot-pink stilettos, which landed catty-cornered near Holly's feet.

"You are not going to believe this," Marla said. Her voice was excited, almost giddy.

Holly had been looking at Marla's light blue toenail polish that seemed even lighter against her dark skin, then she looked up and returned the smile. She lifted her chin and pushed her shoulders back.

"Oh, wait," Marla said. She moved toward the bookshelf behind her desk. "Do you want something to drink?" She opened the small dorm-sized fridge on her bookshelf. "I have Bang, Celsius, Diet Coke, Diet Mountain Dew and Vitamin water."

"A Vitamin water would be great. Thanks."

Marla handed Holly a cold bottle, then moved back to the front of her desk and sat on it. She crossed her long legs at the ankles, started swinging her feet, then leaned forward a little and said, "Bradley Banner has just received the nomination for governor of New York; she's been named as the Democratic candidate."

"Wow!" Holly said as her eyebrows shot up and her eyes grew wide.

Marla nodded. "This is huge for Bradley," she said. "I mean, think about it. She's from a small, rural community in eastern Kentucky. She's like a golden girl." Both of her hands spun, twirling in small circles as her words came more rapidly. "You know, after college she landed a successful modeling career."

Holly nodded as she followed Marla's high-strung info dump.

"And there's her *'In a New York Minute'* talk show," Marla continued. "Which I love, by the way. Even if I don't get to watch it often. Now she has a chance at being governor."

"All of that definitely sounds golden." Holly agreed.

Marla froze in position then, with a serious look said, "I'd like for you to cover this story."

"Wha—"

"It would mean flying to Manhattan this week," Marla said quickly. "There's a press party on Thursday night at some fancy New York restaurant. The following afternoon Bradley's team is hosting some type of fundraiser or benefit. They're calling it the Tulip Tea. It's for her supporters and donors."

"Okay," Holly said.

Marla turned away from Holly and searched through scraps of paper on her desk. She turned back around, then read from a note.

"Thursday-night press dinner is at eight p.m. at Sardi's on West Forty-Fourth. Friday at two p.m. is the Tulip Tea Benefit hosted for Bradley at Kings' Carriage House on the Upper East Side. I just got a call from my New York contact. He owns a PR company in Manhattan and is having to fill in because Bradley's point person has just gone into labor three weeks early."

Marla tossed the note behind her, where it fluttered to a landing spot among all the other notes. "This is your opportunity," she said. "I know you want more responsibility at the magazine and a chance at eventually becoming an editor. So, I want to give you the chance to cover this story. You should be able to get her alone for a few minutes to do a quick Q and A. And . . . " She leaned forward. "I want to put Bradley on the cover of our summer issue. I want to call it 'The Woman of the Year Issue.' I've already made a call to Bradley's people about her being on our cover. In fact, I want Joe to do a cover mock-up and frame it for you to present to her at the Tulip Tea. Our way of officially announcing that she is *Beyond's* cover story and "Woman of the Year" for our next hard-cover issue."

Holly bit her lip as she took all of this in. Before Marla could add anything else, she rattled off her questions as quickly as she could.

"I'm honored to be asked. Really, I am," insisted Holly. "But I have a few questions about getting there, where to stay, if I'll go alone or take a staff member with me. And how much of the expenses will the magazine be able to pay?"

"Valid questions," Marla answered. "I just got off the phone with Gary, and he told me he'd get a room comped for you at The Moxy Times Square, which is in midtown, a great, easy-to-get-to location. He'll pick you up from the airport and will provide transportation to and from your hotel for each event, although I think the first night's dinner is only a few blocks from your hotel. He'll make sure you get to the airport for your flight home. The plane tickets I'll put on the company CC, and your name will be on the guest list for both parties. You don't have to pay for anything, just bring me back a great story," Marla said with a grin.

Marla hopped down from her desk, walked around it, and plopped into her chair.

"I'll email all the details to you this afternoon," she said.

She opened her desk drawer and rummaged around looking for something.

"Here," she said, handing over a credit card. "Book the flight then get this back to me."

Holly took the card from her.

"I appreciate your confidence in me." Holly stood and gave Marla a big toothy grin. "I'm thrilled."

Marla nodded. "And," she said, "once word is out that Bradley Banner will be on the summer cover of *Beyond*, that might be the next big push for us to get primo advertising—bigger companies willing to pay top dollar for full-page ads. You know what that would mean?"

Marla tipped her head to one side, and a look of complete confidence shone across her face.

"Oh," Holly said. "That would be amazing. More money from ads would mean a raise?"

Marla nodded. "Not just a raise, but we would be able to hire a few more writers for our blogs and someone to specifically run our social media so it's not just me. It would be the big break *Beyond* needs."

"Awesome," Holly said.

But she felt anxiety creeping in. Could this really be her big chance to write a cover story, and could the magazine be truly poised for the success they'd dreamed about? Holly stood. Before she turned to leave, she asked,

"Can you make it to team trivia with us tonight?"

Marla shook her head, picked up a prescription bottle, shimmied out a pill, popped it into her mouth, and swallowed it with a chaser of her cotton-candy-flavored Bang.

"I wish," Marla said after swallowing. "Too much to do here, especially with this major story breaking. But soon, definitely soon."

Holly nodded, then walked toward the door. As she reached for the handle, she glanced back at her boss, who was busy typing away on her laptop. Holly slipped through the door. As she made her way back to her desk, she wondered if the others were just as concerned for Marla's health as she was. How long could someone survive on Adderall, caffeine, and a crazy schedule?

3
Team Trivia

"Hurry, get in," Holly said to Stella as they both got into Kali's car.

"Are you sure Marla's not coming tonight?" Kali asked.

"Positive," Holly answered. "Let's go before Wagner or Joe notice we're missing. We can always tell them that we had to get there early to secure a table because I was too busy to make our usual reservation."

"Good plan," Stella commented. "But that's what really happened. You were swamped all day. And stressed out after your meeting with Marla. Since Kali was out on a photo shoot all day, I don't think she's heard the news."

"I guess not," Holly answered. "I will share it tonight. I'll tell everyone during trivia."

"You might also want to share how long you're going to let Wagner swoon over you before you finally tell him you're just not interested," Stella mused. "He asked you out, like, six months ago, and I know that time you had a valid excuse, but he doesn't seem to be fazed by your disinterest."

Holly turned around in her seat to face Stella, who was in the back. She shrugged.

"I don't know," Holly said. "He's really nice, just doesn't seem like my type."

Kali giggled. "So, what's your type? I mean, besides drooling over Timothée Chalamet or that guy from that eighteenth-century show you told us about. What's it called again, and who is the actor who plays in it?"

"Poldark," Holly said. "The main character is played by Aidan Turner. The series is based on books by British author Winston Graham. And I've heard if you go to Cornwall, England, Poldark-themed merchandise and tours are the main attractions."

Holly glanced upward, and a dreamy look appeared in her eyes.

"While my cousin is in England for her performing-arts internship," Holly said, "I might be able to visit her sometime this summer, and we could take a trip to Cornwall."

"Well, there you go," Stella said from the back seat. "If we ever get around to watching this show, we might figure out what Holly's type really is."

Kali snorted. "You mean if she were to time travel back to the eighteenth century."

Holly shook her head and rolled her eyes. "Focus on driving. I feel like I'm riding with the fast and the curious."

Stella giggled. "And drop us off at the door. We'll go in and snag a table while you find parking."

By the time Wagner and Joe got there, the girls had a table, and their cocktails had just arrived.

"You guys took off in a hurry," Wagner said.

"Uh, yeah," Holly answered. "I'm sorry. I got really swamped today and forgot to make our reservation. We had to scramble to get here. You all know how crowded it can get on trivia night."

Wagner smiled at Holly. "No problem. Marla was still in her office when we left. She coming?"

"Nah," Stella said.

Their favorite waitress, Darby, returned to their table to take orders from the guys. And the trivia announcer began giving the usual directions before he listed the categories for the first round. Over the music, the announcer's voice boomed as he called out "Current events, movies, literary figures, and science." Most everyone in the restaurant yelled "Science!" in a jokey, husky tone as was the trivia-night custom.

Kali scribbled down the categories on the team score sheet. Stella and Darby chatted about how excited Darby was to be attending the upcoming Taylor Swift concert at Mercedes Benz Stadium.

"Me and my friends are soooo pumped," Darby said to Stella before moving away to take Joe's drink order.

"Fuck," Wagner yelled, then began typing out a text at breakneck speed.

"Wagner, bro," Stella said. "What's wrong, man?"

"You need to get off your phone," Kali said to Wagner. "Trivia's about to start. You know the rules."

Wagner ignored them and continued his rapid-speed texting.

Darby returned with more drinks. As she set them on the table, she and Stella picked up their conversation about what Darby and her friends planned to wear to the concert.

Wagner put his phone down and scrubbed a hand through his hair. He leaned back in his chair and crossed his arms. His features were arranged in a look of frustration.

"That was Emily Saliers," Wagner announced. "She said she and Amy Ray will have to cancel the podcast interview we're supposed to have tomorrow. They've been booked for a two-night show in Canada, and they have to arrive early to do press, and they'll be leaving town in the morning."

Everyone at the table stared at Wagner and waited for him to elaborate.

"Uh, remind us of who they are," Joe said.

"The Indigo Girls," Wagner answered. "A girl band, a duo actually. They were really big in the eighties and nineties."

"Oh, yeah," Kali and Holly said in unison.

"I've heard of them," Kali added.

"And," Wagner continued, "since they're a local band, it was fairly easy to book them for a spot on the podcast."

"Guys," Stella shouted. "Pay attention. Did you even hear the question?"

"Sorry," Wagner said. "I'm in a serious sitch right now. Not sure what I'm gonna do."

"I heard the question, and I know the answer," Holly said.

"Okay, here." Stella handed Holly an answer sheet and a pen. "Write it down."

"Is this for seven?" Kali asked, wanting to know the point value they were going to use.

"Yeah," Holly answered, then leaned across the table and, in a quiet voice said, "The answer is Linda Yaccarino. The question was who the new CEO of Twitter is. Or X, I have a hard time with the new name."

Kali nodded at Holly, then wrote down the answer and handed the paper to Joe, who rushed it over to the trivia announcer just in time.

When Joe got back to their table, he said, "That's who you should interview tomorrow since the Indigo Girls busted."

"Good suggestion," Stella said.

Wagner shook his head. "I need something fast, someone who would be available without a three-months-out type-of schedule, you know? Although that is a good idea, and I will keep her in mind and see if Marla could somehow work her in for a future remote podcast interview."

Darby arrived, placed more drinks on the table, then took the group's food orders. Stella looked at Darby then back to Wagner.

"I know what Wagner should do," Stella said.

The trivia announcer's voice echoed throughout the restaurant as he gave the answer to the first question.

"Yes!" Holly squealed, then she clapped her hands and high-five-d Joe and Kali.

Stella leaned across the table and snagged Wagner's attention, since he seemed a bit preoccupied and in his own head.

"Wagner," Stella said. This pulled him out of his thoughts and back into reality.

"Yeah?" he answered.

"The Taylor Swift concert is this weekend at Mercedes Benz," Stella said.

"You going?" Wagner asked.

"Next question." The announcer's voice caused everyone to pause and listen this time. "Category, movies. Which movie won best picture at the 2023 Oscars?"

"Easy," said Joe. "Give this one a five. It's Everything Everywhere All at Once."

"We are on a roll," said Kali, marking down a five on the score sheet. Holly wrote the answer down and handed the slip to Joe.

"No, I'm not going to Taylor Swift," Stella continued. "But Darby and her friends are. That's who you should interview tomorrow. Get the college girls' perspective about what makes Taylor Swift so amazing to her fans and her current Eras tour so impressive. Have you broken the news about the Indigo Girls cancelling to Marla yet?"

"Yes," Wagner answered. "I texted her as soon as I found out, but I'm trying to stay off my phone until trivia is over, so I don't know if she's replied or not."

His co-workers nodded. The trivia guy gave the answer to the second question, and the Beyond Amazing teammates fist-bumped each other across the table. Kali lifted both hands in the air, palms facing up, in a 'raise-the-roof' dance motion.

"Next category," Trivia Guy said. "Literary figures. The question is, who wrote the classic titled *Orlando?*"

"Wasn't it Virginia Woolf?" Holly asked.

Wagner smiled at Holly. "Yes," he said.

Kali shrugged. Stella shook her head. "Not sure," she said.

Joe said, "I agree. That sounds right."

"What point value do you want to give it?" Kali asked. "We have a one and a three left."

"What's the final category?" Wagner asked.

"Science!" his teammates yelled together.

"Give it a three,' Holly said. "I'm pretty sure it's right. And we know Wagner won't miss the science question. We'll ace this first round."

4
Winner, Winner

The trivia game was winding down to its final bonus round, and each member of the Beyond Amazing team had finished their second round of beers or cocktails. Just two was their rule on trivia nights—keep it light, keep things tight.

"All right guys," Joe began. "Last round, and we are in second place behind Bane of Your Existence. Let's see if we can pull ahead and win the fifty-dollar gift card tonight. We've been hitting second and third place these last few weeks, and those thirty-and-twenty-dollar gift cards we usually win only go so far."

Holly rubbed her hands together. "Let's do this," she said.

Stella tapped Wagner's arm. "Come on, man. Ask Darby when she comes to bring the checks."

Wagner nodded. "Sure. If Darby and friends don't work, I guess I'll be interviewing Marla tomorrow afternoon."

The announcer started to read the bonus-round question. Everyone at the table went silent. "Out of the top ten longest rivers in the United States, name at least five. Each correct answer is worth five points. So this is your chance to rack up points if you get them all correct." Trivia Guy looked directly at team Beyond Amazing.

Answers were spewed across the table in whispered breaths.

"Mississippi," said Holly.

Kali glanced at the answers Joe had started to write. "Got that already," said, Kali.

"Colorado," added Joe.

"What about Missouri?" asked Holly.

"Good one," Wagner said. "Brazos and Rio Grande. Okay, how many is that?"

"That's five," Kali said. "Did you write those down on the answer slip, Joe?"

"Yep," Joe answered.

After their bonus answer was turned in, Joe returned to his seat, tossed his last french fry into the air, and caught it in his mouth to hoots and hollers from his teammates at the table.

"Hey, I just remembered," Joe said. He looked across the table at Holly. "Aren't you doing an exclusive interview with Bradley Banner in New York, like, this week? 'Cause Marla had me do a graphic with a vector photo of Bradley for the summer-cover mock-up today. She said I needed it to put into a plexiglass frame for you to present or something."

Heads turned in Holly's direction. She nodded. "I almost forgot to tell you guys," she said. But before she could finish, Darby arrived with the checks. And everyone turned to look at Wagner.

"Uh, Darby," Wagner began, "could I ask you a question about the possibility of you and maybe some of your friends being on the Beyond Inspiring podcast?

Darby placed the last check on the table and raised her eyebrows. "I guess so, but why would you want to interview me or my friends? We're just Georgia State University students."

"To be honest, I had scheduled the Indigo Girls for tomorrow, and they canceled last minute. Then Stella suggested that I do an interview with some girls going to the Eras Tour this weekend and do some type of 'everything-Taylor Swift' episode instead."

"Cool," Darby said. "I'm so down for that. When would you want to do it?"

"We usually record the podcast on Wednesdays; we can work around y'all's schedule. Can I get your number? I'll text you in the morning, and you can get back to me with a time that will work. Our office is off of Lenox Road, not hard to find."

"Yeah. I'm out of class by three tomorrow, and my friend Katie is going to the concert with me and Jada this Sunday. I'll text them now and let them know to get back with me about being on the podcast for Beyond. It should be a lot of fun."

"Sounds good," Wagner said.

Darby went about giving Wagner her cell number, then collected everyone's credit cards and their gift card from last week's win. Then she left to finish the transaction while they anxiously waited to hear who had won.

"Fingers crossed," Kali said.

Wagner glanced across the table at Holly. "So, Holly. Sounds like you were given an exciting assignment. Going to the Big Apple this week, huh?"

Holly smiled, nodded, and rocked back and forth a little, before she said, "I'm looking forward to it, that's for sure. I hope I can pull off the story that Marla is looking for."

Wagner returned the smile. "I know you will. When do you leave?"

Before Holly could tell him, the trivia-host began announcing the teams by place. When he finally reached fourth place, the table went quiet. Then third place was announced.

"And in second place, is Beyond Amazing with 92 points. And first place is Bane of Your Existence with 102 points. If your team won, first, second, or third, please come and pick up your gift cards."

Heads fell, and low sighs and groans were heard at team Beyond Amazing's table.

"Bane of Your Existence is just that," Stella said. "Every week that they're here they beat us. It sucks."

The co-workers began to gather their things to leave. Kali went over to the trivia guy's table to pick up their gift card for their second-place win. Joe told the group he was going to the restroom and not to wait up. Wagner hung back, waiting on Holly, who was talking with Stella about what clothes to pack for New York. When they walked to the parking lot, Wagner followed the girls to their car, making sure he stayed next to Holly.

"Stella," Wagner said. "Uh, thanks again for the suggestion for the podcast. I think it'll be interesting. I texted Marla and she agrees it's a great idea."

"Anytime, Wagner," Stella answered. "It's gonna be awesome. Good choice."

"Agreed," said Holly. "Excellent idea. It'll be a good one. Maybe the best podcast idea yet."

Wagner chuckled. "I used to think I was indecisive," he said. "But now I'm not so sure."

He was smiling, waiting for Holly to laugh, but she looked a little confused.

"Just a joke," he said.

They stopped at Kali's car.

"Oh, right. I get it," Holly finally said. She held Wagner's gaze just a tad longer than she usually did. Well, actually she had never actually gazed into his eyes before. She'd never looked at him for any length of time. He'd always been just a bit too nerdy for her tastes. But the way he was looking at her now was so sweet—endearing even. It was the way she wanted to be looked at by a man who was captivated by her, and it made her feel something. She wasn't quite sure what the feeling was. Maybe it was joy, or maybe it was something more intimate.

His dark brown eyes held a glint, a glow, and a sparkle. His eyebrows were nice and neat. His dark curly hair was kinda cute, although maybe it could be styled differently, she thought. One thing was for sure: he'd always been nice to her, polite, and kind. Maybe when she got back from New York, who knew?

"Good night," Wagner said.

"See you tomorrow, Wagner," Holly said before she turned to get into Kali's car for the quick ride from Brookhaven to their office parking lot a few miles away.

5
Ready for It

Once she was seated in Kali's car, Holly pulled out her phone, which she'd put away for trivia, to find five unread text messages. Three were from her cousin, Denim, who was a senior in college and leaving for an internship in London the following week. Denim had enough college credits to graduate with her class, but with this internship, she'd be leaving a month before the ceremony. So over the weekend, her mother and her aunt were putting together a couple of parties for her. The Saturday party would include her roommates in Athens; the one on Sunday afternoon was mostly for family, old friends and former neighbors.

The other two texts were from Holly's mom wanting her to call. The time on her cell said nine thirty. Well, by the time she got to her apartment, it would be after ten. Mom would have to wait, she decided. But before they arrived back at the office parking lot, Holly whipped off a couple of quick texts to Denim, who was so excited about finishing college and starting a theater internship in London but was also looking forward to seeing Holly on Saturday morning.

"Ugh," Holly groaned.

"What?" Stella asked.

"My cousin is leaving college for a special performing-arts internship in London, and my mom expects me to be home for a big event that starts Saturday morning. Mom wants me to come home on Friday. I think she wants me home to help her set up for the parties they've planned, and to be with the family all day Saturday for the activities, the celebration dinner, and my cousin's last theater performance at UGA. Denim and I grew up together; she's like a sister to me."

Holly sighed. "My Mom can really put the pressure on me when she wants me to do something, and I do want to help, but it's mainly because I really want to be there for Denim."

"Yeah," Stella said. "Did you forget?"

"Kinda. I was so stoked, and a little anxious today when I booked my flight to New York. I'm leaving Thursday morning and flying home Friday night, but it's a late-night flight because I have to be at the Tulip Tea benefit on Friday afternoon. I didn't want to push it to rush to the airport with traffic in Manhattan being crazier than here. So I'm going to have to break the news to Mom that I might be arriving later for the family festivities than she wants me to."

"But if you tell her the reason, she'll understand," Kali said.

"Maybe," Holly replied. "Unless she turns into Momzilla, which she's been known to do during stressful party preparations. I'll spring the news on her tomorrow. It's late, and honestly, I can't stomach giving my mom the blow-by-blow details she'll want tonight. You guys know how I've explained my mom to you; she wants to know every stinkin' detail about everything all of the time. She exhausts me."

Kali and Stella laughed.

"Your Mom would love my sister," Stella said. "She loves to tell our mom everything. She's a verbal flowing fountain, spewing information."

The girls arrived back at their office parking lot. Stella and Holly said good night to Kali, then walked together to their cars.

"Will your roommate be able to take you to the airport on her way to work Thursday morning?" Stella asked, knowing that Holly's roommate was a flight attendant.

"No. Lofton left yesterday. She told me she got a European flight because someone needed her to fill in. She won't be home in time. Do you think you could take me?"

"What time is your flight?"

"It's at eight thirty Thursday morning. I should probably get there around six thirty, I guess, since you never know how long the line for security will be. But I have PreCheck, so it shouldn't be too bad."

Stella squinted her eyes thoughtfully as she pursed her lips. Then she glanced at Holly with a conspiring look.

"What if you were to ask Wagner to take you?"

Holly shook her head.

"I'll get an Uber," Holly said. "Good night, Stella."

"Just kidding. Seriously, don't be a friendzilla. But I really think you should reconsider your current opinion of Wagner and maybe ditch your nerd phobia," Stella said, waving goodbye.

* * * * *

The next morning when Holly woke, she remembered she still needed to call her mom.

"Need coffee," she groaned, rolling out of bed.

Padre greeted her with a loud meow, then followed her into the kitchen.

Opening the fridge, she noticed she was still out of her favorite oat milk, not having had time to go to the store.

"Mmm," she muttered in Padre's direction. "I'll just go in early. Maybe Wagner will be waiting with a cup for me."

With that, Padre let out a loud meow as if he agreed that Wagner would have coffee waiting for her. A girl could get used to things like that, Holly thought.

After getting out of the shower, Holly went to her closet to contemplate what to wear. Flipping through a few dresses, she chose a V-neck, T-shirt-style dress in olive green, then she pulled a cropped black leather jacket to wear over it before going back into the bathroom to apply a little makeup and brush her teeth. As she stepped into the bathroom, her phone rang.

"Nooooo." Holly gritted her teeth while looking at her ringing phone. "Hey, Mom," she answered.

"Did you get my message, sissycat? I texted you last night."

"Yeah, Mom. I was at trivia. I was planning to call you today. I promise I will, because I need to tell you some awesome news."

"You're coming home early to help with Denim's party?"

"Uh, no, that's not it. Actually, I'm flying to New York tomorrow for a major assignment. If I can pull off a good interview, I might get the cover story for our summer issue."

"Oh, that sounds good, dear. Who will you be interviewing?"

"Bradley Banner. You know, the *'In a New York Minute'* talk show host?"

"I think I know who you mean. I don't believe I've watched her show. When is it on?"

"She's on every morning from eleven to noon. Look, Mom, I'm going to be really late getting to the office if I stay on the phone. Can I call you later?"

"Of course. You do plan on being home for the party and Denim's last UGA theater performance, I hope. We're expecting you. And I will need your help with both parties."

"I'll call you later, Mom. Gotta go. Love you, bye."

* * * * *

Holly walked through the office doors, halfway expecting to see Wagner walking her way, wondering if his coffee offering from yesterday would become a morning routine. He was nowhere in sight, so she went to her desk, and dropped her bag next to it. Stella arrived soon after that carrying a venti-sized Starbucks cup.

"I need to see if anyone's made coffee," Holly said. "I haven't seen Wagner this morning either. Is everyone running late today?"

"His car is here," Stella responded. "But I haven't seen Kali's car yet. Wagner may be working on questions for today's podcast since he had to scramble with the new program idea. You should have texted me this morning. I would have picked up Starbies for you too."

Holly made a face. "I didn't think about getting Starbies until I saw yours," she said.

Stella shrugged.

Holly wandered off to the staff conference room, which was equipped with a coffee maker and a small fridge for snacks and lunch. After making a cup of coffee, she opened the fridge in search of creamer and flavored coffee syrup. After stirring them in, she had started to head back to her desk when she heard voices coming from the other side of the open-spaced office. From where she stood, she could see Joe and Wagner working on something on Joe's computer. She stood there for a moment, thinking Wagner might look her way. But he didn't, so she went back to her desk.

"You were right," Holly said to Stella when she sat down. "Joe and Wagner are busy working together on something that seems important."

Stella nodded. "Yeah, they need to get the updated podcast information out soon."

A few minutes later, Marla stopped by Stella and Holly's desks. She was wearing a black, tight, knee-length knit dress that showed off her curves, and she'd pulled her dark hair into a high ponytail. Her Nike high tops were hot pink and black and looked way more comfortable than the heels she'd worn yesterday.

"Hey," Marla said. "Would one of you be able to help Wagner out with the podcast today? Kali is on a photo shoot north of the city for a new boutique opening, and I have Joe doing last-minute graphics and layouts for the summer issue. Get this; the new boutique has an actual bar inside the store, and a patio on one side with a window where you can place your wine orders."

"Really?" Holly asked. "How great is that? Wine, shopping, and hanging out on the patio with a refreshing glass of merlot after shopping with your besties."

Marla nodded. "Sounds like the perfect afternoon. Cool concept."

"I'll say," Stella said. "Why couldn't I think of something as genius as putting a wine bar inside a boutique? What's the name of it? Maybe I'll check it out sometime?"

"It's Top KNOTch, located in the new City Center. From here, take 400 North., I think to like, exit fifteen or something. Anyway," Marla continued, "Wagner will only need someone to keep track of the time and signal him at the five-minute mark. You know the drill."

"I'll do it," Holly blurted.

Stella gave Holly a questioning look but didn't say anything.

"Thanks, Holly. You all set for tomorrow?" Marla asked.

Holly nodded. "I believe so. Thanks again for the opportunity, Marla."

Marla smiled. "You got this," she said to Holly. She turned her attention to Stella. "And Stella. Wagner said you came up with the save on the podcast idea. 'Everything T-Swift.' I think this episode will be a big hit," she said before walking away.

6
Swifties

Around four o'clock, three college girls came into the office, each decked out in Taylor Swift Era-themed outfits. Darby looked as if she was representing Taylor's first album, simply titled Taylor Swift, because her dress was a short, shimmery, iridescent, slim-fitting, above-the- knee knockout. She'd paired it with white cowboy boots and put on some large gold hoop earrings. One of Darby's friends had obviously picked the Folklore/Evermore theme and was wearing a plaid shirtdress, wool scarf, and chunky black Doc Martens. Her long auburn hair was woven into a loose braid and as she entered the office, she pulled the braid over her shoulder. The other friend was tall and model-like with glowing mahogany skin. Her outfit was mostly black. This girl had her beautiful black hair slicked back in a tight chignon. Her large dark eyes were accented with thick fake lashes. The simple slip dress she wore was black statin. The look was topped off by a sleek snake necklace, matching bracelet, and was completed with earrings in gold. She'd added bright red lipstick and shiny red chunky-heeled boots. Holly guessed she was probably a fan of Taylor's *Red* and her *reputation* albums.

Stella greeted Darby first. Wagner walked up, and Darby introduced her friends Jada, the dark-skinned, tall, model-looking one, and Katie, the other friend who was wearing the fall plaid. Holly heard the excited voices but stayed to finish her daily blog post before shutting her computer and meeting the others near the entrance.

By the time Holly made her way toward the group, they were seated on the sofa and in the two occasional chairs opposite the couch talking with Wagner. The furniture was from Marla's old apartment, stuff she didn't need after moving in with her boyfriend. It worked well in the large open-spaced office, especially near the entrance.

The office space had high ceilings. Groups of desks were situated on opposite sides of the room. There were only two rooms with doors; one of those was Marla's office, and the other was the conference room. The podcast episodes were recorded in a space that was supposed to be used for storage. The podcast room was like a small walk-in closet and held a round, bar-height table, bar stools for seating, and just enough space for a laptop, microphones, and five or six people seated at the table. Wagner had said the size of the room was great for recording interviews because of its small size and high ceiling.

Darby and her friends were all smiles and giggles. Enthusiasm vibrated through the air as they bantered back and forth with engaging small talk. Holly heard Jada thank Wagner for the opportunity to be on the *Beyond Inspiring* podcast. Her hand lightly brushed his arm as she spoke, her eyes sparkling with interest. Holly took note of this girl's flirtations, and wondered how Wagner would respond. So far, he had been nothing but polite and professional.

"Let's get a few photos before we begin the podcast," Wagner said. He stood first. Then Stella, Darby, and her two friends did the same.

"Where should we go?" Katie asked.

Wagner looked around, then spotted Holly walking toward the group.

"Hey, Holly," Wagner said. "We are going to snap a few pics. Where do you suggest we take them?"

Holly smiled and waved. "I love y'all's Era looks. The pics will be straight fire," she said.

"The three girls said, "Thanks." in unison.

"I think maybe just a plain white-wall background would be best," Holly said and turned to look behind her. "And maybe some fun shots of them together on the sofa."

"Agreed," said Stella. "Definitely some fun shots on the couch. Maybe one of you could be lying upside down, head on the floor, with your feet over the edge of the couch. The other two girls maybe could sit back-to-back and lean against each other while laughing."

"Sounds good," Wagner said and motioned for the girls to follow him to the nearest blank wall.

"I'll go get the ring light," Stella said, walking away.

The dark-skinned girl wiggled her hips and shimmied. "This is going to be a blast," she said, moving closer to Wagner.

Holly could tell that this girl was a huge flirt, and she kept watching Wagner's reaction to her. So far, he didn't seem fazed. And he most definitely wasn't flirting back.

Holly helped pose and position the three girls in front of the white wall. Each of them assumed a model's stance and posed, smiling, with her hands on her hips, placing one foot out in front of the other. Stella returned and turned on the ring light. Jada pulled out her phone and snapped a quick selfie. Wagner captured that on film too.

"Jada," Stella said, "will you do that again, but if you have your lipstick with you, will you pretend to apply it while holding your phone up?"

"Yes, girl," Jada responded. She pulled from her small wristlet a gold tube of candy-apple red lipstick.

Wagner snapped a few more shots. As he took the last one, the girls seemed to be really getting into the photo shoot because their stances turned bolder. Darby lifted the hem of her dress, showing her butt cheek. Katie slid her shirtdress off one shoulder, and Jada crossed her arms in front of her chest, creating even more cleavage while she pursed her lips into a prissy pout.

"Great," Wagner said. "Those will be perfect for the podcast episode image. We'll use some for the link to the podcast on the website and on our blog too. Before you guys leave, we'll get a cute casual one on the sofa like Stella mentioned. And I'll text those to Darby to share with you guys. We'd love it if you used the photos to post about the episode and tag us."

"Absolutely," said Darby.

"So, if you're ready," Wagner said, "we'll go into the podcast studio. Let me warn you, it's going to be a little tight in there."

"That's okay," Jada said, looking directly at Wagner.

Okay, this girl is really after what she wants, and she has apparently decided Wagner is a yummy snack, Holly thought.

As they got situated around the table, Wagner put on headphones then handed Holly the timer and a laptop, on which she refreshed the podcast app. Wagner checked the connection on the Yeti podcast microphone, adjusted a few dials then said,

"I'll do a quick introduction, then I'll let you guys briefly introduce yourselves. Who wants to go first?"

"I will," Jada announced.

Obviously. Holly tried not to roll her eyes or let on what she was thinking. She was also not quite sure why it mattered that this girl seemed to be so into Wagner anyway. It wasn't like she was interested in him for herself.

Wagner began the podcast, then after the girls introduced themselves, he thanked them for being there, then gave a bit of background about Taylor Swift.

"I probably don't need to tell you how successful Taylor Swift is," he began. "But here's just a sampling of her accomplishments. Since the age of fourteen, she's been writing songs professionally. She's won many awards, and forty of them are American Music Awards. She's sold seventy-five million albums. The list goes on and on, but on today's podcast, we want to find out what makes the Eras Tour so special. In fact, it's on track to gross over one billion, which could mean it would be the highest grossing tour of all time, at least so far. To help us understand what makes this tour so successful and what people love about Taylor Swift, let's get some insights from our three guests."

The three girls looked at each other.

"Just dive right in," Wagner said, encouraging any one of them to start. He glanced at Holly, who gave him the time signal by counting out twenty silently with one hand as she kept track, knowing they liked to keep their episodes at a clean thirty minutes. Wagner nodded at Holly. Darby was the first to respond to his question.

"For me," she began. "it's because she writes her own songs, and her lyrics are real; they make you feel something."

"Same," Katie added. "Her songs take you into her life; they lift you up and make you feel better. She's an incredibly talented songwriter and musician."

Holly could feel herself nodding.

"And," Jada said, "she stands up for herself. No matter how harsh the haters are, she remains true to herself, believing in herself, and creating even better music from the low places and dark things she's had to endure."

"Right," Katie said. "Like standing up against that record-label guy and re-recording and re-releasing those old versions of her music so she can get the money for the songs she's written. She's a strong advocate for causes she believes in."

Darby chimed in. "Yes. Over the years she's stood up for things she believes in and speaks out against things she feels are wrong. She won the lawsuit against that guy from the radio station who sexually assaulted her. And she is a role model for young women and young girls. She promotes self-confidence and empowerment."

Jada and Katie nodded in agreement, then Jada added, "She has a strong work ethic too."

"Yes," Darby said. "She's one of the hardest-working women in the music business. And she is a generous philanthropist. She donates to various charities, and she even helps fans in need."

"Should she run for president of the United States?" Wagner asked. He laughed a little. "I'm joking," he said.

But the girls squealed in unison.

"Yes!" they all cried out.

"But only if she wants to," Katie said. "She would make a great president. But she takes her songwriting and music so seriously that I'm not sure she'd have time for anything else right now."

Let's talk a little about your outfits," Wagner said. "I know you guys are excited to go to the Eras Tour this weekend here in Atlanta. Tell us about which eras you guys represent and maybe mention a favorite song or two from those albums."

Darby started. "I'm wearing something that fits her very first album, kinda like original Taylor. She used just her name as the title, and the album was recorded when she was only a teenager. When that first album was released, Taylor's songs had a strong country vibe. It's actually my mom's favorite album by Taylor. My mom's favorite song"—she paused and grinned—"and I like it too, is 'Picture to Burn.'"

"Love that," Katie said, and Jada nodded.

Katie went next. "My outfit is based on the albums she wrote and released during Covid. I picked those because I love autumn and fall weather, and it's also Taylor's favorite season. My favorite song from *Evermore* is *No Body, No Crime*, featuring the female band HAIM. I also love her *1989* album. My favorite from that album is 'Blank Space.' I mean, the lyrics are absolute fire."

The three girls burst into song and sang lyrics from 'Blank Space.' When they got to "Love's a game . . ." Jada looked straight into Wagner's eyes as she belted the words. They cut their rendition short and burst into giggles. Jada composed herself, cleared her throat, and said,

"Well, my outfit is a combo of two of Taylor's albums, *Red* and *reputation*." She sat up straighter and batted her eyelashes a few times (Holly noticed it was in Wagner's direction) before she continued.

"My favorite song from *Red* is 'We Are Never Ever Getting Back Together.' The song she wrote about Jake Gyllenhaal. I think it's hard to pick just one song as a favorite, especially from the *reputation* album. There's 'Getaway Car,' then there's her badass song 'Ready for It?' and 'I Did Something Bad.'"

"You mentioned an actor that one of her songs is about," Wagner stated. "Talk a little about her past boyfriends. She's dated some interesting men. Or so I've heard."

"I *loved* it when she was dating Taylor Lautner," Katie said.

Darby said, "Yes, and she's still friends with Harry Styles. But I think it's hard for people as famous as Taylor Swift to date anyone, especially with the superstars she's dated and their demanding careers and with the press and the general public in your business all the time. And everyone putting you under the microscope, constantly examining every little thing you do or say. That's just gotta be rough."

"I mean, could you even imagine people scrutinizing your every move?" Katie asked.

The girls shook their heads. "No," Jada said. "Dating as a superstar and dating someone who is also a superstar has got to be really hard on the relationship."

Holly signaled to Wagner that he had five minutes.

"Girls, this has been a really fun podcast episode," he said. "I hope you all have a great time at the Eras concert this weekend. Before we go, can you each say something you're looking forward to seeing during the concert?"

Jada and Darby said, "Everyone's Eras fit."

"For sure," Katie chimed in. "And seeing her in person, of course. And trading friendship bracelets with other fans. I've actually made almost fifty of those so far."

Darby fist-bumped Katie.

"The secret song that she'll do just for the Atlanta concerts," Jada added. "At each concert she picks a new song for the set list. Sometimes she gives little Easter egg-type hints of what those songs might be."

"I love trying to figure her secret fan codes out," Katie said.

"Thanks, ladies," Wagner said. "And, as always, we'd love for you to show the *Beyond Inspiring* podcast some love by giving us a rating, a like, and a follow."

With that, Holly stopped the recording, and Wagner removed his headphones.

"Okay, ladies, thanks again," Wagner said. "Let's get that last fun photo on the couch before you guys head out. And I'll text Darby the link to the show once I've finished the edits."

"I'll be glad to give you my cell number," Jada said, moving closer to Wagner as they walked back into the main part of the office.

Unbelievable, this girl, Holly thought. But she also tried to ask herself why it mattered that someone was flirting with Wagner.

"Um, sure, yeah," he stumbled out.

"Do you need me for anything else, Wagner?" Holly asked.

Wagner smiled at Holly. "You did great. I appreciate it. Thanks, Holly. Just gotta work on edits."

Holly nodded and began to walk away, but she was still watching as the girls moved to sit on the sofa for the photo. Katie posed upside down, her head on the floor with her feet slightly draped over the edge of the couch. Darby sat next to Katie with her back to Jada. Jada leaned back against Darby and threw her legs over the arm of the couch, raising the hem of her skirt.

Holly quickly turned and walked back to her desk.

"Ugh." Holly sighed and rolled her eyes. *Would Wagner be the type to fall for a girl who is an insatiable flirt?"* she thought.

7
NYC, Here I Come

Holly picked up her bag, turned to Stella, who was also gathering her things to leave, and said, "Hey, I'm going to speak to Marla before I head home. She's got the cover shot framed that I'm supposed to give to Bradley Banner."

"You need me to do anything while you're in New York?"

"Nah," Holly answered. "I'm sure you'll be busy doing double blog duty while I'm gone. But I would love it if you'd pack my suitcase for me. I still have to do that tonight."

"Am I still picking you up tomorrow around six, or did you get a ride with Wagner?" Stella joked.

Holly closed her eyes, shook her head, then with a grin, she looked at her friend. "You're funny and the best. See you in the morning."

As she and Stella walked toward the entrance, Stella rushed over to speak with Darby as she walked out the door. Katie followed, and Holly watched as Jada reached out to grab Wagner by the elbow just as he started to walk back to the podcast room. Holly heard

Jada say, "I just wanted to thank you again. This has been so much fun. I look forward to getting the photos and the link soon."

Holly walked quickly past the two of them before she could hear Wagner's response and knocked lightly on Marla's office door.

"Come in," she heard from deep within the office.

When Holly walked in, Marla was on her Peloton bike, which was in the far corner of the room. Marla was peddling fast with sweat dripping from her face, and her phone was propped up near the bike's screen. She was obviously on a call. After Holly had waited a minute, Marla ended the call, wiped her brow with the towel hanging on the bike's handlebar, then stepped off.

"Michael didn't want to haul this bike to the office for me," Marla said. "But I'm so glad he did. It's just so cool being able to work out while you work, ya know?"

"Sure, yeah," Holly responded. *Marla's boyfriend is a great guy to put up with all of Marla's requests,* Holly thought. "I just wanted to say that I'm heading out now. My flight leaves at eight thirty tomorrow morning, and I'll be home around midnight Friday, but I will need to leave first thing Saturday morning to drive home. I mean, to my parents' house. My cousin is leaving for London, and there are parties on Saturday and Sunday. Lots of family stuff going on this weekend. When do you want me to submit the story and any photos I take?"

Marla shrugged. "Just as soon as you can. I'd love to see at least a rough draft on Sunday. Do you think that would work for your schedule this weekend?"

Holly's stomach clenched. Anxiety started to creep in, but she pushed it down, and with a cheerful voice said, "I will do everything I can to get it to you on Sunday. Oh, and do you have the mock-up cover for me to take?"

Marla walked over to a six-foot plastic folding table, where she'd laid out advertising for the upcoming summer issue, and the mock-up cover was sitting, framed, next to all the ads.

"Here," she said, picking up the chunky, beveled-edge plexiglass-covered image and handing it to Holly.

Holly looked at the framed cover of *Beyond* featuring a photo of Bradley Banner. The copy next to it read, "Woman of the Year."

"Well, I guess that's it," Holly said. "I need to pack. Have a good rest of the week. Try to take it easy, Marla."

Marla lifted her hand in a goodbye as her phone began to ring again. Holly slipped out the door, where she ran straight into Wagner. Her breath caught in her throat.

Holly took a step back but not before she caught a hint of his fresh scent. "Oh, Wagner, sorry."

Wagner was all smiles. "No problem. You headed out?"

"Yeah. Guess I'll see you next week."

Wagner held Holly's gaze. Maybe he wanted to say more. He stammered a little when he said, "Uh, right. I . . . um. Have a great time in New York. I look forward to hearing about it."

He moved away from Holly and knocked on Marla's office door. Holly could hear Marla yell "Come in" as she made her way to the front entrance.

* * * * * *

Back at home, Holly pondered packing. She stood in her closet and picked out some items and was setting them aside when her phone rang.

"Mom," she said. "Shoot, I forgot. I told her I was going to call her back." She slid her thumb across her phone screen to answer. "Hey, Mom. Sorry. I forgot to call you."

"I know you did, dear. That's why I'm calling *you*."

"Well, the good news I wanted to share is that I'm flying to New York tomorrow to do an important interview with Bradley Banner. I think I might have mentioned that. I've got a real cover story this time."

"That's wonderful. When will you be home?"

"I'll be at Denim's on Saturday. This is just an overnight trip. My plane gets back to Atlanta around midnight on Friday."

"Oh my gosh, Holly. Who will pick you up at the airport? Do you have a male friend who could drive you home? I don't feel comfortable with you doing one of those Ubers so late at night."

"Uh, yeah, Mom. I have a friend picking me up."

Although Holly had not actually thought about who would be picking her up until her mother mentioned it. Should she ask Wagner? Nah. It would be so late, and she wasn't even really friends with him. What would he possibly think about her if she were to ask? Would he think she was interested in dating him? She should see if Lofton would be home and make her drive to the airport at midnight to get her. Lofton owed her that. After all, she was never home with the way her flight-attendant schedule had been lately. And, Holly had been taking such good care of Lofton's cat. Poor kitty.

"Are you listening, dear? Did you hear me?"

"Uh, sorry, Mom. I'll see you on Saturday, okay?"

"You need to call me when you land. And then call me before you leave on Saturday morning. You know how worried I'll be."

"Can I just text you, Mom?"

"Oh, that's fine. Please be careful in New York. Don't step out into traffic; they'll just run you over, then I'll see it on the news with the headline 'Young Girl Run Over by Yellow Cab, Body Crushed by Pedestrians.'"

"Mom you are killing any New-York-City vibe I had. I need to go. I'll see you this weekend. Bye."

"Don't forget to text me."

Holly hung up, tossed her phone onto her bed, and decided to curl up with Padre and watch something on Netflix before she drifted off.

In the morning, she packed three dresses, a T-shirt, jeans, essentials, and her makeup bag into her carry-on. She'd chosen a few of her favorite heels, one pair she hadn't had a chance to wear yet, but they screamed, New York City. She added the shoes before zipping up her carry-on. Into her large tote she stuffed her laptop, her camera, and a small crossbody bag. Then she took the plexiglass framed cover and added that to her large tote. She picked up the bag, took the carry-on by the handle, and was starting for the door when Padre ran out in front of her.

"Hey, boy. You almost tripped me. Your mommy will be back tomorrow."

She reached down to give his head a scratch. Her phone dinged with a text from Stella letting her know she was waiting outside.

* * * * * *

At the Delta terminal, Holly told Stella she'd text her later. She walked inside and was grateful to get quickly through the PreCheck line and past security without having to wait very long.

She made it to her gate just as priority seating was being called to board. There was an empty seat near the edge of the line, so she sat down and wished she had made time to get coffee. She wouldn't be able to board until the last group was called because her seat was toward the back, but she didn't want to risk missing the flight.

Finally, it was her turn. *I hate walking past all of these people through the entire airplane,* she thought. It felt as if all eyes were on Holly as she made her way toward the back of the plane. She prickled at having to squeeze past people and wedge herself into a seat next to strangers. *What would it be like to sit in first class? Maybe one day I'll find out,* she thought.

As she arrived at row thirty-five, she looked around at all the closed overhead compartments. *Surely, they can't all be full.* But they were. She had no place to put her bag, and she was stalling and holding up the line of people who had seats in rows thirty-six through fifty.

A flight attendant signaled to her. "You can give me your carry-on bag," she said.

Holly tossed her large tote into the middle seat, which—yay for her—was *her* seat, squished in between two strangers. She then rolled her carry-on to the very back, where the flight attendant was waiting. More people began to follow her with their bags in hand. Soon Holly was standing with six strangers in the small, cramped space where the flight attendants stored snacks. Holly wondered how long they would be huddled there. Seven suitcases were piled in one corner, and one of them was hers. More bags came rolling down the aisle toward where she was standing. This overcrowded situation might have been hilarious if it were a story being told by a friend, but while it was happening in real time, Holly was anything but amused. It was beginning to feel like something from an SNL skit in which she'd gotten trapped in a sarcastic scenario. An image of being stuffed into a tin can full of sardines was starting to take shape.

The flight attendant asked everyone for their seat numbers and wrote them on Delta cocktail napkins, which she put on top of their respective bags. Holly wondered if she should be impressed by the ingenuity of the flight attendant using napkins as labels and stepping up to the plate, since it was apparent this crew was not prepared for the number of bags or limited space. Or should she be mortified at the thought of possibly never seeing her bag again? Two more bags were added to the pile, and the flight attendant added a numbered napkin to each.

When the aisle was almost clear of people, the flight attendant assured Holly's group, still scrunched into the cramped space, that their bags would be checked and waiting on the carousel at LaGuardia. Holly took one more glance at the numbered Delta cocktail napkin sitting on top of her suitcase, then decided what the hell and went to sit in her seat. She was thankful the flight was less than three hours, because what was the protocol for the armrests in the middle seat?

Maybe it wouldn't be an issue, because the older man and woman on either side of her seemed totally nice, like people who clapped when the plane landed. She just prayed she wouldn't need to get up to use the bathroom.

Once they landed, Holly made her way quickly to the carousel to wait for her bag. She moved as close as she could get to the circulating contraption and looked at each bag as it made its appearance on the rotating track. Nothing yet. She scooted to the side and stood directly in front of where the bags entered the track, and she watched and waited. Soon, she saw hers was about to pop down, but instead it got stuck.

"Nooooo," she whispered.

Other bags were falling onto the circulating belt past hers, which was still stuck sideways like a bumper car waiting to get knocked back into the rink. If only another bag would hit it and knock it loose. *Come on, you can do it. Just hit the corner just so. Come on.* So far, no luck. *Am I going to have to climb in there and knock it loose myself? If I do go after it, will I fall forward onto the carousel with my feet in the air, sprawled across the thing like I'm a drunk? Would I be caught by airport security and held in a locked room, waiting for some type of interrogation?*

As her thoughts about how to get to her bag consumed her, a large suitcase came out and tapped her bag at the corner just enough to knock it down onto the rotating device, where Holly gratefully reached for it. She hoisted her large tote over her left shoulder and pulled up the handle on her rolling bag. Then she looked around for the exit where she'd wait for her ride. Before she started for the doors, she checked the text message she'd received earlier about where to go and what color and type of car to look for.

I think his name is Gary, she remembered as she walked outside to find the number painted on the column where she was to wait. She looked for the red Toyota van that was supposed to be there but didn't see any red vehicles. Just then her phone rang.

"Hello," she answered.

"Holly?" the girl asked.

"This is Holly."

"Awesome. I'm supposed to pick you up, and I just wanted to make sure you were in the right spot."

"I'm at the green column with the letter *"C."*

"Perfect. I'm pulling up now."

Holly hung up, and within a minute she saw the red van pull up. The driver double-parked in front of where Holly was standing. A blonde girl about her age got out and opened the sliding van door for her.

"I'm Brianna, but you can just call me Bree. Garrison was busy, so he sent me to pick you up."

"Thanks. I thought someone named Gary had been texting with me."

"I think some call him Gary, but his full name is Garrison. I usually call him that, but you have the right person. Garrison handles publicity for a lot of events in the city, and he's actually originally from Atlanta. He's your contact."

Holly nodded and got into the van, then Bree pulled away from the curb and into the crazy New York traffic. Horns honked, people cut each other off, brakes slammed. All the chaos you could think of happened at once as Holly tried to focus on the scenery.

"It's getting close to lunchtime," Bree said. "I bet you are starving. Do you want me to stop and get you anything?" she asked.

"No, I'm good right now. But thanks."

"Tonight's event doesn't start until eight. You could even be a few minutes late. It's kinda the fashionable thing here, to be a little late but not too late."

"Gotcha."

"You'd definitely have time to do some sightseeing."

"Sounds good. I'll try to do that. Would you recommend taking Uber, or should I take the train?"

"Honestly, the train might be faster; this traffic can be a real pain sometimes. And you could walk even faster, depending on where you want to go. If you want to do some shopping, there are trains just a few blocks from Bergdorf's and Tiffany's, and your hotel isn't far from Macy's in Herald Square. Those are some of the typical touristy areas people enjoy seeing. Just pull the subway map up on your Apple Maps app. Type where you want to go, and the app will show you what color train to use."

About forty minutes later, Bree pulled up in front of The Moxy hotel near Times Square.

She parked in front then said, "By the way, this hotel has an awesome rooftop bar. But you need a reservation, and those can be hard to get, and impossible at the last minute. Just have Garrison call one in for you. It's rocking up there until at least three a.m."

"Wow, okay. Thanks again," Holly said as she exited the van.

8
Sights and Sounds of NYC

Even though it was only around noon, the boutique hotel had a room ready for Holly on the sixteenth floor. After getting settled, she began texting with Stella, and Stella told her that Wagner said to tell her hi. Next, she sent a text to her mom letting her know that she'd arrived, then Holly decided to do a little sightseeing.

She grabbed her coat since the late-March temperatures, although the day was sunny and clear of clouds, were only hovering at around fifty degrees. She opened her Apple Maps app and typed in where she wanted to go. *First, how about a walk through Central Park*, she decided, then headed for the nearest subway station to board the yellow line toward Fifth Avenue and the famous park.

As she walked through the crowded streets, the smell of cannabis hung thick in the air, which reminded her of every Atlanta music festival scene she'd been part of. Passing the famous Tiffany's flagship store, she couldn't help but stop to gaze at the window displays. One window beneath the Tiffany-blue awnings showcased what seemed like magical blue boxes of crystal stemware for the most elaborate table setting. Another window featured flowers upon flowers of gorgeous bouquets dripping with sparkling necklaces and earrings snuggled among the colorful petals. *Next time I'm here,* she thought, *I'll go inside. Who knows? Maybe if this cover story really becomes what Marla thinks it will be, I'll get a raise and even be able to buy something from here.*

At the next corner, she saw Liberty Bagels, and since she still hadn't had lunch, she wandered inside. A display of the most monstrous, enormous bagels drew her further inside, where the next glass cabinet showcased over twenty flavors of cream cheese, from peanut butter to strawberry to honey bacon to lox scallion. The flavors were piled high and looked somewhat like scooped ice cream. It was like something from a bagel-lover's dream. Finally, she decided on an everything bagel with strawberry cream cheese, which she asked them to toast since she enjoyed a crispy bagel. She paid, took her enormous bagel, and walked across the street, past the tall gold statue at Grand Army Plaza and the beautiful Pulitzer Fountain and on toward Central Park.

In the park, so many people were out walking their dogs, running, or just hanging out with friends. Holly stopped to watch the turtles at the lake before following a path up to a bridge. Along the way she noticed a tranquil sunny spot near the water, and in the grass a couple had spread out a large quilt. On a low table they had set out a lovely display of candles and flowers. They were leaning against plump pillows, feeding each other apples and cheese. It was perfectly romantic and picturesque and looked like something from a movie.

Wagner's face came to her mind as she watched the couple for a brief moment. She shook her head and walked past the lush grassy meadow, feeling confused about why the happy couple had made her think about him. She'd never before thought of him in a romantic way. In fact, she'd rarely ever thought of him at all. Had Stella's advice to give Wagner a second look actually gotten to her?

Farther into the park she came across an advertisement from the Museum of Modern Art promoting a Taylor Swift exhibition. Holly pulled up the museum's website on her phone to see the hours and price, then made a quick decision to go. *Why not? I have plenty of time until my event at eight, and it's only six blocks from where I am now. It would be crazy to be in New York for twenty-four hours and not try to squeeze in something fun.*

After spending an hour looking at Taylor Swift's rhinestone guitars, original song lyrics, and handmade custom costumes—exhibits that would thrill any Swiftie—Holly decided it was time to take the subway back. On the way to the train, she remembered the rooftop bar above her hotel. Bree had mentioned that her boss, Garrison, could make the reservations for her and supposedly get her in regardless of the crowds. She whipped off a quick text to the number Bree had texted her that morning.

This is Holly Curtis, Could someone make a reservation for me for later tonight at the Magic Hour rooftop bar at The Moxy Times Square?

By the time she got off the train near Thirty-Sixth Street, she'd gotten a response.

Done. It's at eleven forty-five tonight. I was only given two options and the other was at 12;45 a.m. Show them this card on your phone when you arrive. The reservation is for two people. Wasn't sure who would be going with you, but your name is on the reservation.—G.S.

Below the text message was an image of a business card. The letters *G* and *S* were bubbled and large, surrounding part of an outline of the New York City skyline like a giant balloon. The information below the image said, "GS Events NYC, LLC. Promotions, Marketing and More." A website was listed along with a phone number and a P.O. box. In smaller letters below those was a name, Garrison Simmons. The name was familiar, and Bree had mentioned earlier that her boss was from Atlanta. *Nah, it couldn't be him, but what if it was?* she wondered.

Thank you, **she texted back.** I hope to meet you tonight. I appreciate everything, the car service, and the hotel.

A thumbs-up emoji was all she got in return. *He's busy, I'm sure,* she assumed.

When Holly got back to her hotel, it was almost six thirty and cocktail hour was happening on the second floor. She thought she'd check it out to see if there was anything to snack on. She stepped off the elevator and into what appeared to be a party. A DJ was set up across the room playing sick beats, and people were sitting and hanging out throughout the bar. As she made her way up to the shiny copper-topped counter to order a drink, the bartender asked if she was a guest of the hotel. She told him her room number, and he said she had a thirty-dollar credit that would be taken off at checkout. He took her order and began making her drink. She'd ordered "The Moxy," which was made with dragon fruit and gin. The bartender handed Holly the fruit-topped glass, and she wandered over to a large table decorated with cute individual charcuterie cups.

She picked up a cup and started to nibble on some cheese. She looked around for a place to sit, but most of the sitting areas were full, so she decided to take her drink and charcuterie cup to her room. After all, she needed to get ready for the press party, and she most definitely wanted to look the part tonight, not only dressed for success but like the prominent journalist she hoped to become.

9
The Famous Sardis

Holly checked her appearance in the full-length mirror in her small hotel room. Her black dress fell several inches above her knees, and the short, ruffled sleeves stuck out like wings, giving the dress a sophisticated appearance. She added Anne Klein low pointed-toe, kitten heels in black-paten. Her makeup was more daring than usual, and she'd even put on fake lashes. She picked up her black leather Michael Kors crossbody bag and her coat. Since it was only about seven thirty, the sun hadn't fully gone down, so she thought the eight-block walk would be fun and would give her more time to see the sights. Later, on her way back to the hotel, or actually to the rooftop bar, she'd definitely use the car service.

On her walk she paused at Herald Square and took in the lights. Times Square was all aglow in the early evening shade. She looked at her phone to make sure she was still on schedule to be fashionably late but not too late, as Bree had suggested.

When she arrived at Sardi's, there was a mass exodus of diners spilling onto the sidewalk, and she wondered if there was a fire. Soon she realized that those were people who had show tickets, because she watched them walk across the street and into the Shubert Theater, where the musical comedy *Some Like It Hot* was playing.

After the groups of people were gone, Holly walked inside and was stopped by someone wanting to check her coat. She took off her coat, handed it over, took the ticket from the lady, and slipped the orange paper into her small crossbody bag before making her way over to the hostess stand.

"Are you here for the private event?" The maitre d' asked.

"I am. I'm Holly Curtis with *Beyond* magazine."

He nodded and said, "The party is up these stairs." He pointed to a staircase on his left.

Holly made her way upstairs to the second floor. What she noticed most about this interesting restaurant were all the framed caricatures of famous people. They covered every inch of wall space. Once she got to the landing at the top of the stairs, she could see that even the walls on the second floor were covered in portraits. She made her way to the hostess stand and told the young girl working there her name. Holly noticed the logo on the girl's black button-down shirt. There was an embroidered image that was the same as the one on the business card she'd been texted earlier. The bubbled letters *G* and *S* encasing part of the New York skyline were embroidered in red on the left side of the girl's button-down.

The girl ran her finger down the list in front of her. Then she called another girl over who wore the same black shirt with the logo.

"I can't find this lady's name on the list," Holly heard the girl say to her co-worker.

The co-worker looked at Holly, who by this time was feeling a little funny, unsure, and maybe a bit nervous.

"Are you a guest of Ms. Banner? Or are you with the press?" the co-worker asked.

Holly shook her head. "Uhm. No. I'm a writer. I'm with *Beyond* magazine."

"Oh, right," the girl said. "There's another list on a different sheet. I think Garrison said he put it here on the shelf. Both girls dipped their heads to look on the shelf inside the back of the hostess podium. "Found it," the co-worker said. "And here." She pulled out a bag. "They are supposed to get a lanyard that has their name and their company written on the tag." She handed the bag to the first girl.

That girl dug into the bag, looking for a lanyard for Holly, while her co-worker found her name on the new list.

The girl handed Holly her tag once her name had been found.

"I'm sorry for the confusion, ma'am," she said. We are short-staffed tonight. The one who normally does this job called in sick last minute."

"It's fine," Holly said, taking the lanyard from her. "Thank you."

A line was forming behind Holly, so she moved to the side to slip her lanyard over her head. From where she stood, she could see groups of people, cocktails in hand, chatting, some with animated hand gestures and others with boisterous laughter.

There was a bar to the far left near a wall of windows that reflected Broadway lights and looked out onto the busy street below. Holly decided she'd get a drink for liquid courage. She made her way toward the bar, through the maze of tables, as the room grew more crowded by the minute. She saw an open spot at the bar and moved in that direction as a tall man in a dark suit passed her. He wore a red tie with a matching pocket square. His dark hair was slicked back. Holly watched him as he greeted guest after guest. When his head turned just so, she couldn't deny it. He looked just like the very same Garrison Simmons she'd had a crush on her freshman and sophomore years in high school.

Suddenly she felt her stomach drop like something from the top of a New York skyscraper. Would he recognize her? Did he already know it was her? I mean, he had her name. He'd made arrangements for her to be picked up at the airport; he'd even made a reservation for her and her invisible friend at the rooftop bar for tonight. How much had Marla told him about her when she said she was sending someone to do the interview and cover story for *Beyond?* She stepped up to the bar and waited for one of the bartenders to notice her.

As soon as a bartender asked what she'd have, Holly said, "A Pimm's Cup."

It was all she could think of, being as nervous as she was after seeing her former heartthrob. Her mom and her aunt had practiced making Pimm's for Denim's London-themed party, and she knew how excited her mom was to show off her English-cocktail expertise. The bartender handed her the drink, topped with a lime, then added a small black straw. After she took the first sip, she heard the tap-tap of a microphone, then Garrison Simmons. in his expensive-looking suit, gathered everyone's attention.

"Ladies and gentlemen," he said, "if you would please find a seat anywhere you'd like, it will be my pleasure to introduce our special guest of honor for tonight."

Everyone moved from the bar to find seating at tables throughout the room. As people passed Holly, she noticed many of the guests had lanyards now. Some of the names she spotted were *The New York Times*, Condé Nast, ABC, NBC, CNN, and Fox News. Tables were filling up fast. Holly grabbed a seat at a small table quickly. An older lady sat next to her and introduced herself as Lydia. Lydia commented on how pretty Holly was. Holly didn't recognize the organization listed on Lydia's lanyard.

"What news outlet or publication are you from?" Holly asked her.

Lydia smiled. "Oh, I'm not with the press. I'm the president of a local women's group here in the city. It might not be anything you've ever heard of. And what about you, dear?"

"I'm a writer for *Beyond* magazine. It's a new women's magazine, and, it's based in Atlanta."

Lydia nodded. "Wonderful," she said.

Then Garrison gathered the crowd's attention again. Holly couldn't help but notice how strikingly handsome he looked.

"Ladies and gentlemen, members of the press, and special guests, it is such a pleasure to host your next New York governor. Please put your hands together and join me in welcoming Ms. Bradley Banner."

Hoots and cheers broke out along with loud applause as Bradley made her way from the staircase into the room. Behind her were five more people making up her entourage. The crowd stood as she entered, and the applause continued. She made her way over to Garrison and gave him a hug, then he handed the microphone over to her. Holly sat back down once she noticed everyone else was sitting. She watched as Garrison made his way toward the back of the room and stood near the bar. Holly sipped more of her Pimm's.

"Thank you," Bradley said. "I am honored to be with you all this evening. It's going to be a rough ride, filled with hard work, and the campaign could get tricky. But I'm going to give it my all, and with your backing and your support, I know we can make progress and move the state of New York in the right direction with a promising future with me as New York's next female governor."

More applause broke out, and Bradley waited for it to end before she finished her speech.

"I want to meet each and every one of you this evening. I'm here to learn what you all have to say." She paused as light cheering erupted. "You don't need me to tell you what you want from the state government. Instead, I'm here to listen, to learn, and to take into consideration your ideas for New York. My campaign starts here, and moves to Long Island, then up the Hudson Valley, stopping at major cities along the way. Then we'll end it in Adirondack Park for a two-day conference."

More applause. Bradley smiled at her captive audience. She was beautiful. Tall and gracious. The grace she had developed during her days as a model radiated from her. Her golden-blonde hair was piled atop her head in a striking updo. Her beaded blue gown was slim-fitting and shimmered in the light. Once the applause ended, she continued.

"I'll continue with my talk show, *In a New York Minute*, so most of my campaign travel will be done on

Friday afternoons, Saturdays, and Sundays. And with my talk show, I'll be adding a segment with interviews of statesmen and other government offices throughout the state which I think will help us all to gather informed information on the needs and issues throughout the state of New York. It will focus, too, on certain topics that need to be discussed, and it will shed light on important issues that could lead to making New York the best it can be. So my campaign won't be limited to only meeting people in cities and towns; I'll be working daily to learn as much as I can. Thank you again for being here."

Garrison stepped up and took the microphone from her. Someone from his staff must have shown Bradley's entourage where to sit, because they were seated at a table near the hostess stand, and a server was delivering a meal to their table.

"Servers are coming around with food," Garrison explained. "Bradley will be making her way to you at each table. Feel free to order more cocktails. And enjoy the evening meeting Bradley and taking photos. One of my staff members will be walking around to get pictures with Ms. Banner. If you want one on your phone, perfect. Our staff will be glad to assist with that as well. Enjoy your evening. 'Banner is better. 'Banner is best, and 'Banner is the bold new face of New York!"

When the applause died down, Garrison and Bradley made their way to one of the tables closest to where they had been standing. One of the girls who had helped Holly at the hostess stand was now the official photographer. Holly needed to make sure she got photos on her phone as well once Bradley made her way over to her table. And what about Garrison—would he be stopping by each table with Bradley? Should she remind him of how they knew each other, or would that be weird?

Holly had a few minutes to ponder this since there were many tables for Bradley to stop at before getting to hers. And, thankfully, a waiter was walking toward her table with a bread basket and plates of pasta or steak. It looked like she would get to choose an entree. She asked for the pasta and requested another drink as more liquid courage was definitely needed.

10

The Night is Young

Lydia was chatting with Holly about her new beach house in Montauk. It sounded wonderful, and although Holly was interested in the conversation with her table companion, she really needed to focus on being prepared once Bradley made her way to their table. When Lydia moved the conversation to her interior decorator's boyfriend, Holly decided it was time to get Lydia on a different topic.

"Tell me why you are supporting Bradley Banner for governor," Holly said. "And if you don't mind me quoting you in my cover story for *Beyond*, I'd certainly appreciate it."

"Absolutely," the older lady said. "It's time New York had someone like Bradley as governor. She's a great people person. I've been a fan of hers for years, ever since '*In a New York Minute*' first aired. It's time for the momentum to continue, to keep a woman in office and show that it's no longer a man's world. And Bradley has the guts and the grace to lead our state. I truly believe she does."

Lydia gave Holly more insight into the state's economy and specific needs as well as tax-related issues, and Holly recorded everything with her voice-memo app. Before she knew it, Bradley was taking photos with the people at the table next to them. Lydia grew more excited and asked Holly to make sure she snapped a good photo of her and Bradley with her phone, especially if she planned to use it for the article. She also asked Holly to make sure she got her good side. Lydia reapplied her lipstick, and Holly decided to do the same. The next thing she knew, Bradley and Lydia were shaking hands and photos were being snapped. Holly took a few photos on her phone first then took some with Lydia's phone before setting it back on the table. Holly stood up, ready to meet Bradley and introduce herself, and as she did, she felt someone watching her closely.

"Holly Curtis?" Garrison asked as his eyes bored into Holly like laser beams.

Holly smiled and lifted her shoulders a bit. "It's me," she said.

Garrison was all smiles. He'd always had the perfect smile, Holly thought. White, straight teeth and a big smile that filled his entire face. Up close he had a five-o'-clock shadow. He smelled incredible, his dark eyes glistened, and he seemed very happy to see her.

"I had no idea you were Marla's New York contact," Holly said. "She called you Gary. And I really thought I had been texting with some dude named Gary." Holly laughed.

Garrison laughed too. "I know. Same here. I mean, I knew your name was familiar, and I thought of you, and I wondered, Could it be?"

"It really is me."

The photographer interrupted Garrison and Holly to ask Holly about photos with Bradley. Holly looked away from Garrison to see that Lydia was thanking Bradley and moving back to her seat at their table.

"Yes, please," Holly answered. "Garrison, could you take some with my phone too?"

He nodded. "Of course."

Holly handed him her phone and moved next to Bradley for a quick photo shoot. Once the photos were done, Holly introduced herself to Bradley. Garrison was still holding Holly's cell phone.

"We are thrilled to have you on the cover of *Beyond*, Ms. Banner," Holly said.

"I'm thrilled and honored to be on your cover," Bradley said.

"I'm writing the cover story," Holly added. "If you don't mind me asking a few questions. I know you still have more tables to get to first."

"Yes, I'd love to answer all of your questions. Why don't you find me, once people start to leave, then you can ask away."

Bradley looked at Garrison. "What time do you think we'll be wrapping up here?"

Garrison looked at his watch. "It's almost ten, so I'd say in about an hour."

"Come find me then, Holly," Bradley said.

Garrison gave Holly a smile. He winked at her then gave her phone back. When Bradley turned to greet the next table, Garrison whispered to Holly, "I'd love to talk with you some more too."

A jittery jolt hit Holly in the stomach. Was it because her former crush had winked at her? Or because he wanted to talk with her some more—or both? Holly nodded then sat back down to finish her meal. Waiters were bringing desserts around. A few people who'd already spoken with Bradley were starting to leave, but most were enjoying themselves, and Bradley still had more tables to get to. Holly took out her small notebook and reviewed the questions she wanted to ask Bradley, and pondering what Garrison might say to her and what she might say to him.

11

Intrigue and Interviews

Lydia left shortly after their dessert arrived, saying it was way past her bedtime and her driver had returned. She asked Holly to send her a copy of the summer issue of *Beyond*. And had given Holly her Montauk address, where she'd be spending the summer. Holly told her she'd be glad to mail her the issue. After Lydia left, more groups started to make their way downstairs, but there were still others hanging around. Some who'd had way too many cocktails were waiting on their rides. Holly watched as Bradley wrapped up a conversation with a couple and moved toward her entourage. Garrison was speaking with his employees, and soon afterward his staff members left. Holly decided to make her way over to Bradley to see how much she could get done for the interview. Whatever she got tonight would be added to the details and comments at tomorrow's event as well as any photos. She also planned to mix a short biography of Bradley into the cover story.

Bradley ended her conversation when Holly approached.

"I'm all yours," Bradley said. "Let's sit."

She pointed to the empty table next to her. Holly sat next to Bradley and pulled out her phone.

"Do you mind if I record our conversation for the interview?" she asked.

"Not at all. Please go right ahead."

Holly opened her recording app and pressed the button. "First," she began, "I'd like to ask when it was that you knew you wanted to run for governor?"

"Not long after I moved to the city. Being here allowed me so much personal growth. It's almost as if I came to life here. New York City is vibrant." Bradley spread her hands flat onto the white tablecloth. Her long nails matched the blue of her dress. She leaned toward Holly. "You probably know I come from a small town in eastern Kentucky. And after winning Miss Kentucky in the spring of my senior year in college, I got the opportunity to travel and develop my platform."

Holly was nodding along following everything Bradley said, but out of the corner of her eye she watched Garrison as he led the last of Bradley's supporters toward the staircase. When he turned back around, his eyes met Holly's. He smiled, waved, and mouthed the words "I'll wait for you." Another strong flutter flip-flopped in Holly's stomach. *Could this be like something from one of those cheesy Hallmark movies? Rekindled sparks flying between her and the one perfect boy she'd been crazy for but could never have in high school? Was a romance possible with the almost-forgotten hometown boy from her youth?*

She shook away those thoughts and pulled her attention back to Bradley, who was talking about women's issues and the nonprofits she'd worked with over the years. She continued to describe the way those interests had led to service on the boards of several New York nonprofits supporting women and children. That in turn had ignited her desire to run for office if or when she thought she might have a chance to do so.

The conversation moved to her early days as a New York resident. "After my year as Miss Kentucky, I received the offer to move to New York and model for Victoria's Secret. I already knew their costume designer who specifically designed for their Angels runway show. He had designed several costumes for my pageants over the years." Bradley smiled. "I actually looked up who had designed the themed costume for Miss USA to wear in the Miss Universe pageant, and that's how I found him. I wanted only the best designer. Better costume, better chance at winning, and all that. Once I'd graduated, he put in a good word for me. I got an interview, and a trial photo shoot, and things went from good to great. After I started my modeling career, I got involved first with The New York Women's Foundation then later the Children of Promise nonprofit, and after serving on both of their boards for many years, and after retiring from the world of modeling. . ."

Her voice trailed off. She paused, smiled at Holly, and glanced at her entourage, who were chatting quietly at the table next to them, then turned back and continued her thoughts. "By that time, I'd met some people who were willing to give me the opportunity to host my own talk show. That, of course, gave me the chance to promote, support, and continue to help those nonprofits and shed light on women's issues like economic justice, safety, healing, empowerment, race issues, and mentoring. For that I feel very lucky, and I'm grateful. My talk show, *In a New York Minute*, really gave me a platform to highlight some of the needs I'd now like to address in the race for governor. It allowed me the opportunity to bring important issues to the table, to host guests who could shed light on topics I felt were important, and talk about areas where change was needed."

Bradley paused and met Holly's eye. "What I'm about to share is something that really needs to stay off the record because you never know what type of information your opponent will use against you in a political race. Those close to me understand this about me, and I think it's something that is important to understand about me personally." Bradley held Holly's gaze for a beat. "When I received the call from Marla about being selected 'women of the year' for the magazine, she told me she was sending her most enthusiastic, trustworthy reporter." Bradley smiled. Holly nodded, and a sense of pride washed over her from knowing Marla trusted her. Bradley continued, "One day, I plan to move back to eastern Kentucky, and when I do, I want to run for governor there. But for now, with the platform I currently have, New York is where I feel I need to be. Saving the world is something I can do one step at a time, or one state at a time, I should say."

"That's interesting," Holly said. "And I very much understand how that is something personal to you that you feel strongly about. I certainly wish you all the luck in the world with your upcoming endeavors—most importantly, winning the race for governor." Holly laughed. "I know my vote doesn't matter, but I sure am pulling for you. I think you answered my next questions already— what distinguishes you from other candidates and why you decided to run. So let me ask this: Did you have previous political experience or experience holding an office or working with a large budget?"

Bradley laughed. "Well, I ran for president of my sorority in college and won. I had been treasurer prior to winning the role of president, and before I was the treasurer for Tri Delta, I'd held committee positions. Those might not involve large budgets, but they did mean working closely with other women and making things happen as a leader and as a team player."

"What would be your goals after winning the governor's race, say after thirty to ninety days of being in office?"

Bradley's expression turned serious. "We need to address and try to stop the flow of fentanyl into our communities. We need to stabilize the police community and offer better training to new recruits. To reduce gun violence. We need to address mental-health care and help provide for unmet medical needs. Raise the minimum wage and provide more affordable childcare options. And to work on New York's housing crisis and encourage housing growth."

Bradley paused and met Holly's eyes. "Those are just a few of the top items that will be on my agenda."

Holly nodded. "Those are excellent initiatives. I believe I have a start to a good article. Thank you so much for your time. I'll be at the Tulip Tea benefit tomorrow afternoon. In fact, I have a surprise that I'd like to present to you during that event."

"Wonderful. It was nice to meet you, Holly. And I'm really thrilled to be on the cover of *Beyond*. Marla was so kind to suggest the cover story for your next issue. In fact, once the issue releases, I'd love to have Marla on the show." Bradley stood, and when she did, her entourage followed suit.

Holly's eyes lit up. "She'd love that, I'm sure."

Holly turned off the recording, placed her phone and her small notebook back into her purse, then stood, and held out her hand to Bradley, and they shook. Bradley and her group stopped to speak with Garrison briefly before they made their way down the stairs and out to their waiting limo. Holly made her way toward the restroom but was stopped by Garrison.

"Do you have plans now? Or plans with someone?" he asked. His eyes danced over her face with interest.

Holly smiled at him, and she felt butterflies take flight in her stomach. "I have a reservation at the Magic Hour rooftop bar at my hotel, which you kindly made. But no one's coming with me."

"Can I give you a ride? I would love to hang out with you a little longer. That is, if you'd like to."

"Yeah, sure. I was just headed to the restroom. But I'm game to hang out."

"Meet me downstairs when you're done. I'll have my driver take us to Magic Hour."

Holly walked into the restroom and bent over to catch her breath. *This is really happening,* she thought. *Okay, Holly, don't get too carried away. Stay cool. You're just going to hang out with him. Catch up like old friends; this is no big deal. It's not like he was your dream guy or your biggest crush in high school.* But, actually, he was.

12

Magic Hour

When Holly got to the bottom of the stairs, she saw Garrison waiting, and he waved her over. Once they stepped outside, Holly realized she'd forgotten her coat and went back in to get it. She stepped up to the coat-check window and handed over her ticket. As she slipped her coat on, she pondered what she was doing. Was leaving with Garrison a good idea? But her more adventurous side told her it was. After all, he was a successful businessman who owned his own PR company in New York City. She'd crushed on him all through high school and had voted for him when he'd been selected student-government president their senior year. Always popular and smart, he had been in the National Honor Society with her, and he was still very good-looking, maybe even better-looking now that he was in his midtwenties. What did she have to lose? She wasn't currently dating anyone, and it might be a lot of fun to catch up with an old high-school friend, crush or not.

Most importantly, she was curious. She had always wondered what it would have been like to have gone on a date with him, even though hanging out with him tonight did not constitute an actual date. Still, she was intrigued, and what better way to find out what he was really like than to go and enjoy an evening with him? Would she even be gutsy enough to tell him she'd had a crush on him? And if she were to tell him, what would that lead to? Well, the night was young, and romance seemed to be in the air, and what better way to savor her twenty-four hours in New York than with a new opportunity? Garrison held the door open for her, and together they walked out onto the busy sidewalk.

He placed a hand lightly on Holly's arm and made a gesture with his other toward the right. "One of my drivers will pick us up at the corner of Forty-Fourth and Seventh. It's just easier for him to get to," he said.

Holly smiled and walked with him. The temperature had dropped since she'd arrived, and she pulled her coat tighter and buttoned the top two buttons. When they got to the corner, Garrison's driver was waiting.

"This is us," Garrison said, opening the back door of a black Cadillac sedan.

He held the door open for Holly, and she slid into the back seat and across the slick, cool leather to the other side. The driver turned and said "Hello." Holly acknowledged him then clicked her seatbelt. After Garrison got in and closed the door, he said,

"Holly, this is my driver, Rick. Rick, this is Holly."

"Nice to meet you," Rick said. "How was your event?"

"It went well," Garrison replied. "Everything was smooth. Can't ask for more than that. Can you drop us off at Magic Hour? Stay on Seventh and just drop us off at the corner of Seventh and Thirty-Sixth."

"Sure thing," Rick answered.

The ride was super quick, and Rick pulled up at the corner to let them out. As soon as he did, the driver behind him laid on the horn. Rick ignored the angry driver, but Holly knew it would completely drive her insane if she had to deal with the chaos of driving in New York traffic. Garrison stepped out of the car and held his hand out to Holly. When she stepped out of the car, she could see a long line down the sidewalk. Garrison walked straight up to the front and spoke to the bouncer. The bouncer opened the gate and waved them through, and they walked up to the hostess stand. Garrison showed the girl at the stand his business card and ID, then told her they had a reservation. The hostess pulled up the information on her computer screen, looked at Garrison's card, then told them to go on through.

Garrison placed his hand on Holly's lower back and guided her further through the doorway. They walked through a narrow tunnel with lights flashing pink and purple, then around a corner and through a maze of mirrors. Finally, they came to the elevator and stepped inside, and Garrison pushed the button for the eighteenth floor.

When they stepped out of the elevator, they walked through another hallway and into a foyer, where another hostess led them to their table. The roof was closed due to the cold temperatures, but because it was made of all glass, the city's nighttime lights shone through. The New York skyline was lit up all around them. In front of them, a small carousel rotated slowly, and Holly watched as groups of people hopped on and off to snap photos with the Empire State Building in the background. A DJ was spinning beats, and the music thumped and radiated with surrounding spotlights. The sounds vibrated in Holly's chest. Their table was close to the bar but on the other side were amazing views of New York City at night.

"This place is really cool," Holly said.

"It's nice," Garrison commented. "Especially with views of the Empire State Building because it's so close. But there's an even nicer rooftop bar with more panoramic views of the city. Maybe not as kitschy as this place with the carousel and the mini golf." He pointed to a corner, where Holly saw a giant pink-bunny statue and glowing lights spelling out 'Fore Play.'

"Mini golf. How fun," Holly said. "Where is the other place with better views?"

"It's a nightclub called Somewhere Nowhere. The actual bar area often has live music. And it has a great jungle or wildflower theme with exotic birds. Not real ones, but tropical birds are just part of the themed décor. You have to go up a few more floors to the rooftop. I think it's, like, the thirty-ninth floor. Up there is a smaller bar, less noise, cozy seating. It even has a small swimming pool, and there are panoramic views. It's on top of the Renaissance Hotel near Chelsea."

Holly nodded. A waitress arrived and gave them menus.

"I'll let you look these over," she said. "I'll come back in a few."

As Holly read the drink menu, she giggled.

"Oh gosh," she said. "The names of these drinks are too funny. Mr. Pink, The Momager, Sliving. I definitely feel like I'm sliving right now. Slaying and living my best life. And the Moira Rose." Holly sat back a little, lifted her chin, and quoted the character from a popular TV series with a dry, snooty, flamboyant voice. "I'm positively bedeviled with meetings, et cetera."

This cracked them both up. " Good one," Garrison said. "You sound almost just like the real character, Moira Rose. And—" He paused, set his menu down, and said, "It's great to see you. Really, Holly. I'm glad we can spend more time together tonight to catch up."

His expression was serious but also held a hint of curiosity.

"Yeah, me too," said Holly.

The waitress came back and asked if they were ready to order.

"I think I'll have the Moira Rose," Holly said.

"I'll have The Fix," Garrison said. "And could you bring an order of truffle fries and the vegetable crudités?"

"Of course. Coming right up." The waitress scribbled everything down then left.

In no time the waitress was back with their drinks. Holly's drink was quite impressive. A large, red rose-shaped ice cube sat in the bottom of a martini glass. The waitress slowly poured bubbly pink liquid over it, and the red rose floated to the top.

"So pretty," Holly said.

"Your food will be out shortly," the waitress said and left again.

Garrison loosened his tie and unbuttoned the top button of his shirt, then he lifted his cocktail glass. "To old friends," he said, then tapped his glass with Holly's.

They both sipped their drinks. Holly sipped a little more.

"This is so good," she said before setting the martini down.

"You know," Garrison said, "I might have had a slight crush on you."

Holly looked at him. She was shocked. She sipped more of her drink.

"I know it was a long time ago," Garrison continued. "Like, when we were in high school. Sophomores or something. But I remember asking you for your number and looking forward to talking to you in honors English. You were funny from what I remember, and you always had a great meme to share with me. And you were cool, really laid-back, not worried about what people would think about you. I really liked that you had your own ideas and unique opinions."

Holly's stomach fluttered. This is what her younger self had heard in her daydreams, things she'd wished he would have said to her back then. She smiled at Garrison, not sure how she should respond. She sipped more of her cocktail as she pondered. Maybe she should be honest with him and tell him that he was her high school crush too. The waitress arrived with their food. After she placed the dishes in front of them, she asked Holly if she'd like another drink. Holly finished off the last sip then nodded.

"Sure, why not," she said.

The waitress nodded at her, and set a stack of napkins with the Magic Hour logo on them down then turned to leave.

Holly turned and faced Garrison, who was nibbling on fries.

"I was starving," he said. "When I work dinner events like the one tonight, I never have time to eat. Please help yourself. I promise I won't eat everything."

"Okay, thanks.," Holly said. "And congratulations by the way. Not only on tonight's event but on the business you've built. It's successful. And you live here in New York City. That's fabulous. But with all of your accomplishments in high school, I always thought you were someone who was bound to be a success. I mean, you were the freakin' homecoming king."

Holly's comment made them both laugh. Garrison almost choked, coughed a little, wiped his mouth with his napkin, then said, "Glory days for sure."

He grinned, and his soft brown eyes landed on hers. A smile broke out across her lips. Holly was feeling a lot more at ease with Garrison—so much at ease that any doubts she'd had about him earlier had vanished.

"Thank you," he said. "It also depends on what you deem as success."

Holly took a bite of guac and chips from Garrison's vegetable plate, which also consisted of several types of sliced vegetables with a vinaigrette dipping sauce. She nodded, chewed, and kept her eyes on Garrison.

"Look at you," Garrison said, opening his arms wide with his palms open. With both hands, he gestured toward Holly. "You've got the cover story for a new trendy Atlanta women's magazine. I'd say you are on your way."

Holly and Garrison's second drinks arrived. Holly sipped on her fresh cocktail. With more liquid adrenaline, she might be able to share her feelings for Garrison. Maybe this really could be a second-chance romance with a handsome heartthrob. She might even be able to write her very own tropey rom-com after tonight. But she reined in those thoughts, not wanting to get too carried away with what might happen between her and Garrison just yet.

"I know you went to the University of Georgia after high school," Garrison said. "Did you major in journalism?"

Holly shook her head. "No. I majored in marketing, but I minored in creative writing." She laughed. "I wanted to make sure I was good at writing slogans, jingles, and one-liners. Like Don Draper from *Mad Men*. I know he's a fictional character from an old TV series, but man, he could pull a great slogan out of thin air like nobody's business."

Garrison chuckled. "I've heard that show is a good one. Never watched it though."

"What about you?" Holly asked. "You went to Georgia Tech after high school, right? What was your major?"

"Yeah, I started out at Tech in business administration. As a freshman, I joined a fraternity, and some of my brothers decided to start a band. I played keyboard. We played a lot of gigs those two years I was with them, but it started to get a little wild, and I wasn't as focused as I needed to be on school. I mean, yeah, I could have graduated from Tech and gotten a good job somewhere in Atlanta. But I wanted something more. I needed a change of scene to get me back on track and more focused on my studies. So I transferred to Columbia here in the city right after my sophomore year. I started summer classes and even got an internship at a PR company. Then I started planning and saving for the business I wanted to start."

His hand brushed against Holly's when they both reached for more snacks. Their eyes met. They held each other's gaze for what seemed like a lifetime although it was mere moments. Garrison placed a hand on Holly's knee. Her stomach leapt into her throat.

"I'm glad you're here," Garrison said. "I'm glad we've met up again and at a different time in our lives."

The look in his eyes was inviting. His hand on her knee was gentle. The sound of his voice was soothing. After two cocktails Holly's liquid courage had kicked in.

"I had a crush on you too," she blurted.

Garrison's features glowed in the dim lights of the bar. His eyes searched Holly's.

"I was never sure if you did," he said.

"We talked so much during English class," Holly began. " Flirted too. It was the highlight of my week. Even before having a class with you, I'd liked you. Then at the end of that year, after you finally asked for my number, summer vacation hit, and you texted, like, once or twice. The next thing I heard was that you and Kimberly Wilson were dating. She was beautiful and the most popular girl in school. I gave up any hope after that."

Garrison looked crushed. He shook his head, then rubbed his forehead.

"Ugh. Yeah, I was a jerk, I guess. Kim and I ended up seeing each other at Rosemary Beach that summer. Our families had rented houses near each other. It just happened." Garrison grinned at Holly. "You had a crush on me too, huh?"

The waitress came around to check on them, and they decided to order a bottle of sparkling water and desserts. After all, interesting things were just getting started.

"You wanna dance?" Garrison asked.

"Sure," Holly said with a glance in the direction of a group dancing near the DJ.

Garrison shed his jacket and tie, laid them next to Holly's coat, and unbuttoned the top two buttons of his shirt. He took her by the hand as they made their way over to the dancing group and mixed in with them. The music vibrated through Holly. The steady, pulsing beat of the techno version of the song had her moving and bouncing, her inhibitions gone. She let her guard down and moved closer to Garrison, and soon their bodies melded together as they swayed along to the music. The New York skyline and the lights from the Empire State Building glowed around them. The low, hazy lights of the bar, encased in the glass ceiling, with the shimmer of New York City at night, made Holly feel like she was in a bubble—a magical one.

13

Feel the Beat

Garrison pulled Holly closer as they danced. The song changed and the tempo slowed. Their movements became more subtle. Holly wrapped her arms around Garrison's neck and breathed in his spicy, smoky, leather-scented fragrance. His five-o'clock shadow grazed her cheek. Garrison turned his face to meet Holly's so that their lips were just inches apart. Holly felt a pull like a magnet tugging her mouth toward his. Garrison tipped his head, and his lips met hers like a soft pillow. She opened her mouth, and his tongue dipped inside slowly and gently. As their kiss deepened, Garrison's hands rested on either side of Holly's hips, holding her in place. But when he gripped her ass, Holly stopped kissing him. She pulled away, coming out of a drunken fog, as she realized they were making out on a dance floor like teenagers on prom night, and she suddenly felt very self-conscious.

Holly took Garrison by the hand, and they walked back to their table. When they moved to sit down, Garrison sat next to Holly on the bench seat and moved in close, then he wrapped an arm around her, pulling her to him.

"I like your hair," Garrison said. "Shorter suits you."

"Mmm. I always thought guys like longer hair on girls."

"It depends, I guess," Garrison replied. "Younger guys might not be thinking with their brains and definitely not running on all cylinders. But the way the light is reflecting off your short blonde waves with the city lights behind you, it's quite beautiful."

Holly turned and looked at the Empire State Building behind her, pulled out her phone, and snapped a selfie. A lot of the photos she'd taken since she'd arrived in the city earlier in the day had been selfies. She looked at the screen and thought the photo looked cool with the skyline peeking from behind her, so she posted it to her Instagram. She added a quick, cute caption then set her phone on the table. Soon her phone started blowing up with notifications, and within a few minutes a text popped up. Garrison noticed the text, but Holly just flipped her phone over since the notifications were becoming a distraction.

"Are you seeing anyone back in Atlanta?" he asked.

"No," Holly said. "Should I be asking you the same thing?"

Garrison shook his head. "No. I'm not seeing anyone."

"I deleted my Bumble account," Holly said. "I just didn't like the vibe. I guess I prefer to meet someone in person versus just swiping across a screen and randomly landing on someone who matched. People can hide behind their phone screens. It's like they can be more anonymous. It's as if people can live in two different realms. The way they want to be perceived and what they say online can be a lot different from who they are in real life."

Garrison nodded. "I know."

"In person," Holly continued, "people show more restraint, more patience, and I think you see who they really are much better than from behind the screen. I think we are shaped by our experiences, and those happen in the real world. So I'm going to hold out with the hope of meeting someone special in the real world from now on. Speaking of which . . ." Her thought trailed off and she looked at Garrison with a flirtatious smile.

Garrison returned Holly's smile and leaned in, giving her a quick kiss, and he whispered, "How much are you holding out for?" When Holly didn't respond, he leaned back against his seat then said, "I can see how people would show more restraint in person versus through a screen." He paused. "Unless you're driving around New York. Then you might have to yell at someone with something like, 'You have the attention span of ice cream in July,' or 'You're the reason the gene pool needs a lifeguard,' or some other wisecrack with a little more profanity involved." This made them both snicker. "Are you a fan of the show Catfish?" Garrison asked. "I used to watch it. Crazy stuff went on. But sometimes the person they were talking with ended up being actually legit, and it worked out."

"Yeah, I know the show. I used to like watching that too. I've actually done a little research, just from wondering about dating apps and being curious about people getting duped or scammed. There's a guy out in California who created a service called Social Catfish. It started as a blog to educate people about online scams and catfishing. But today it's more of an investigation tool. I've thought about interviewing someone who works for Social Catfish for the *Beyond* blog."

Garrison smiled. The hand that he had around Holly's shoulder moved up to her neck, and his fingers lightly danced across her skin just below her ear. It gave her tingles in the best way.

"Smart, talented, and beautiful," he said.

He leaned in and kissed her gently, his lips lingering on hers. Holly responded to the gentleness of the kiss and returned it with the same sweetness. It felt as if someone was doing back flips in her stomach, and she let out a soft moan as the kiss grew more passionate. Garrison slipped his other hand between Holly's legs and slowly moved it up her thigh. Holly reached down and stopped his hand from moving further, then broke the kiss. Their eyes met. Garrison grinned and leaned in to kiss her again, but Holly didn't return it, so Garrison kissed her cheek instead.

Garrison's forwardness seemed out of place. After all, they'd just been reunited and were getting reacquainted. It wasn't like they were on a date. Surely, he didn't just assume she was going to hook up with him because she'd shared that he'd been her high school crush—he couldn't be that entitled and arrogant. She tapped her phone screen to look at the time.

"Maybe we should ask for the check," Holly said. "It's getting late. It's after two in the morning. And I don't know about you, but I've had almost five cocktails tonight, and that's a lot for me."

"Sure," Garrison said. It's easy to lose track of time when you are having a great time. And not wanting the night to end. Can I walk you back to your room?"

"That would be nice, but, of course, not necessary."

Garrison downed the last of his drink, and within a few minutes, their waitress walked by, and he asked for the check. Holly got out her credit card and set it in front of Garrison.

"We can split it," Holly said.

Garrison shook his head. "Nah, let me get this."

He picked up one of her hands, brought it to his lips, and placed a light kiss on it while holding her gaze. It seemed very chivalrous, but it also made Holly giggle.

"I appreciate the gesture. Really, I do. Thank you, Garrison. But let's split the check."

"Look," Garrison said. "I don't want you to feel like you need to offer to pay. I invited myself because I wanted to catch up, to spend some time with you. And let me be honest. I'm really, really glad I did."

He moved Holly's card toward her. She shrugged, picked it up, and placed it back into her wallet.

"So, maybe I'll hit you up on Instagram," she said.

Garrison grinned. "You mean you've unfollowed me since high school?"

Holly raised an eyebrow. A smug look crossed her face.

Their waitress arrived with a handheld device that allowed them to pay their check. Garrison paid, picked up his tie, draped it around his neck, tucked his coat under one arm, and waited as Holly put on her crossbody bag and coat. Once they started toward the elevator, Garrison placed a hand on Holly's lower back as they walked side by side. When they were alone on the elevator, he pulled her toward him, cupped her face with both hands, and kissed her like he meant it. The way he kissed her made Holly woozy. It was soft and passionate, and she thought she could kiss him like that for endless hours. When they got to the street level, he walked with her inside the foyer of the Moxy hotel and then onto the elevator that would take her to her room.

"You don't have to come up with me. I'll be okay."

Garrison shook his head. "I'm sure you will be fine. But I want to."

As the elevator began to move, Holly asked if Garrison would be the one to pick her up tomorrow and take her to Kings' Carriage House for the Tulip Tea.

"I'll have to look at the schedule for tomorrow," he said. "I'll do that in the morning. Either way, you will get a text from me or one of the company drivers. Your name will be on the guest list like tonight. Someone will probably pick you up between one thirty and one forty-five. I made sure you had a late checkout when I got the room for you."

Holly nodded. "Thank you for thinking of that."

The elevator opened and they stepped out and walked together down the hallway to Holly's room. She stopped at the door and pulled the key card from her bag.

"Garrison, thank you again for tonight. It's been fun seeing you again. And——"

Before she could finish, Garrison pulled her to him. His arms slipped inside her coat and wrapped around her waist. His lips met hers with a feverish passion. He was a great kisser, Holly thought. They had attraction and chemistry, not to mention that they'd had a little too much to drink. Holly gave into her passion and kissed him back with the same fervor. Garrison's hands moved down to cup her rear, then one hand slipped under the hem of her dress. His other hand moved to her right breast. When she felt his fingers slide her underwear aside, she pulled away quickly, shocked by what felt like an assault.

"Garrison, I don't think . . ." she started while tapping her keycard to open her door, but Garrison put his hand up to stop her. She felt fear at that moment. Was he going to push his way into her room? Just then, an older couple came down the hall, walking past Holly and Garrison.

"Good night, Garrison," she said rather loudly. And she quickly unlocked the door, pushed it open, then closed it, leaving Garrison in the hallway.

Without hesitating, she pulled out the safety latch and locked the extra deadbolt. She leaned her back against the door and let out the breath she'd been holding. She turned around and looked out of the peephole. Garrison was rubbing his forehead, a look of frustration on his face. She continued to watch as he pulled out his phone. Was he about to call her? He lifted his hand like he was about to knock, then decided otherwise and turned to leave. She stood there for several minutes waiting and listening for any sounds or movements. When she heard nothing, she finally moved away from the door.

Her phone buzzed. She went to sit on her bed and with trembling hands she pulled her phone from her purse and looked at the screen. She had two texts; the most recent was from Stella saying she had seen the IG pic and commented on how gorgeous Holly looked and that she hoped Holly was having a great time in New York. The other was from several hours ago, and it was from Wagner, who just wanted to see how things were going and to say hi.

She thought about calling Stella, just to chat. Maybe she'd feel better if she spoke with her friend about what had just happened. Or maybe she was being too easily offended, too sensitive; it might be nothing. She could be overthinking. Garrison could have just gotten the wrong idea. Had she led him on? But she decided no, of course she had not led him on. They'd only kissed, and there was no reason for him to have been so forward. He had most definitely overstepped. Garrison had taken advantage of her. It's not like they were a couple, and even if they were, he should at least have asked if it was okay before assuming she was just there for his pleasure. He had no right to take from her what she might not be ready to give.

She plugged her phone in to charge, then reached for an unopened water bottle, unscrewed the lid, and took a long drink. It was almost three a.m. She went into the bathroom, washed her face, brushed her teeth, and slipped out of her dress before heading to the bed and crawling under the covers. Maybe Garrison would apologize tomorrow, she thought. Maybe he would beg forgiveness. Maybe they'd both gotten carried away, or maybe he just wasn't the prize prince she'd thought he was. She squeezed her eyes shut and asked God to keep her safe and for sleep to come quickly.

14

The Tulip Tea

Holly woke to the buzz of a text message. It was from her roommate, Lofton.

Hey girl, got home and saw your note. NYC, how cool, and for a cover story. Let's celebrate once you're home. Maybe at The Garden Room at the St. Regis? Anyhoo. Yes, will pick you up tonight around midnight.

Holly replied to Lofton, then looked at the texts from Stella and Wagner that had come in last night, or actually early that morning. She "liked" Wagner's message. Then she texted Stella that she had so much to chat with her about later. It was twelve thirty, and she needed to shower and pack her bags to get ready for the Tulip Tea. She wondered if she'd hear from Garrison or if she'd see him at today's event.

Her feelings about his behavior last night had not changed. He'd overstepped and assaulted her sexually, and that was something she'd tell him. Because having known him in high school and actually having enjoyed catching up with him last night made her think that there was a good guy in there somewhere. Could it be that he just needed to be schooled on how not to be a jerk while on a date? Or on what was appropriate and respectful? After she explained it all to him, if he still acted like an asshole, well, that would be on him. Either way, he'd get her lecture, and she'd let him do with the information as he pleased. Whether he was a good guy or bad, she was going to give him a piece of her mind if she saw him later today, of that she was sure.

By the time she got out of the shower, she had a text message waiting for her from Bree.

Hey Holly, Garrison asked me to pick you up around 1:45 today. I'll drop you off at Kings' Carriage House on the Upper East Side. You will be able to leave your luggage in the van. Afterwards, I'll drop you off at LGA airport.

Thx, Bree.

She set her phone down and couldn't help but wonder if Garrison was avoiding her.

* * * * *

Later, Bree arrived at the Moxy, picked Holly up, and drove her to her destination. Parked in front of the red-brick Kings' Carriage House was a small white vintage van that had been turned into a custom drinks cart. Painted on the side was 'Parked Prosecco.' A long vine of ivy, mixed with various types of flowers, flowed in graceful tendrils from the roof down to the front tire, where the impressive arrangement puddled on the ground. Through the open window of the van, Holly could see the bartender mixing drinks. Waiting patiently and chatting was a line of elegantly dressed women in stiletto heels and large feathered hats cocked precariously to one side of their heads.

After last night, Holly decided she needed a cocktail about as much as she needed a blister on each one of her toes, which were now squeezed inside her brand-new pair of heels. They were incredible-looking shoes, but sometimes beauty came with a price. Although gorgeous shoes might not be a requirement as much as comfortable ones were, these were definitely a welcome accessory Holly had decided she needed in her wardrobe. Squeezing past the line of ladies, she maneuvered her large tote to the front of her body to avoid bumping into anyone on her way to the entrance. Once inside, she was greeted by a hostess who asked for her ticket.

"I'm sorry," Holly said. "I don't have an actual ticket."

The girl looked at Holly, puzzled. "Ma'am, the Carriage House tea rooms are closed today for a private event. We'll be open for lunch tomorrow."

"I'm actually a journalist. I work for *Beyond* magazine, and I'm covering this event for an article. Maybe Garrison Simmons left my name with you?"

Holly was beginning to sweat a little. What if Garrison was really angry, and she was about to be denied entry? But the hostess pulled a sheet of paper from the podium.

"Tell me your name," the hostess said.

"Holly Curtis."

"We have all of the press seated together. Please sit at table twenty-eight."

"Thank you," Holly said and continued into the room.

Maybe the girl at the door thought Holly wasn't there for the tea because she wasn't wearing a fancy Kentucky-Derby-style hat. Whatever. She'd obviously not noticed Holly's floral ankle strapped Betsy Johnson heels, which seemed perfect for today's event. Maybe Marla needed to make special press badges for her Beyond employees to proffer like FBI agents do whenever they wanted to get into private events. Those might be kinda cool.

The room was filled with small round and square tables. Each had seating for three to five guests. More sharply dressed women in hats and fascinators stood around, talking in small groups. As Holly made her way through the room, she looked at each seating arrangement for her number. At the center of each table were beautiful ceramic teapots filled with sumptuous yellow tulips. Sticking up above the tulips were numbered cards on long gold sticks. Finally, at the far back of the room—basically in the hallway—she found table twenty-eight.

A girl around Holly's age was standing next to the table when Holly walked up. Holly pulled out a chair and set her large bag down on it. The girl turned and spoke.

"Hi, I'm Kirkland. I'm with the *Times*, and you?"

"Hey, I'm Holly. *Beyond* magazine."

Kirkland extended her hand, and the two young women shook.

"There are a few more here too," Kirkland said. She tilted her head a little to the right. "Reporters and journalists, I mean. They've put us all at the same table. The others went to snap a few photos of the silent auction. That's in the next room. Want to walk in there with me?"

Holly shrugged. "Sure. Just curious, though. Did you and the other journalists have tickets to get in today?"

Kirkland shook her head. "No. Why?"

"I was stopped by the hostess at the front door, is all. So I was just wondering if I'd missed something somehow."

"The rest of us got here before there was anyone at the front. Good timing, I suppose. It also depends on who's handling the PR for the event." She laughed. "A good press contact will have prepared the staff with the names of the journalists planning to be at the event. Hopefully they already had your name."

"Yes. I told her who I was, and then she pulled out the list. But I'm curious about the cost of the tickets. I suppose everyone else needed one to get in, and these ladies are dressed as if they are about to greet the King of England and his royal court."

"Aah." Kirkland nodded then stepped closer to Holly and whispered. "This benefit for Bradley Banner is being put on by The Colony Club."

Kirkland waggled her eyebrows.

Holly shook her head in slow motion.

"Doesn't ring a bell," Holly told her. "But I live in Atlanta and am here to report on Bradley. She's our cover story for our summer issue."

Together they moved into the next room.

"Gotcha," Kirkland said. She leaned toward Holly. "The club is exclusively for women and was founded in 1903." Kirkland held a hand over her mouth then said. "It's expensive to be a member, like really expensive. And, you have to be invited to join by someone who's already a member. The Colony Club has its actual headquarters, or whatever, a few blocks from here on Park Avenue. And they have a strict protocol on seating. Their membership has rankings, especially when it comes to being seated at events. The oldest members or maybe the wealthiest—not sure—are seated near the front. They always put the press who covers any of their events in the back of the room."

"Interesting," Holly said.

In the next room were tables lining all four walls, and women were wandering past, examining the auction items. The offerings were divided into sections. One table was full of jewelry, including some from Tiffany's, David Yurman, Kendra Scott, and Julie Vos. On another table were gift cards for restaurants and stores like Macy's. Another table had books autographed by authors, and still another held designer handbags. The girls wandered through, looking at each item.

"Look at this one," Kirkland said. She picked up a small Gucci handbag. "How cute is this?"

To Holly, the striped pastel bag looked like a carton of rainbow-sherbet ice cream. It was nice, but definitely not something to easily pair with most outfits. And for the price of a bag like that, she thought, it better go with everything she owned.

"What's the latest bid on that one? Is it a lot less than retail?" Holly asked.

"Mm-hmm. The latest bid is one thousand."

"Definitely not going to bid on that," Holly said.

Kirkland put the purse down, and the girls continued to browse. They came to the first table in the room, which they'd somehow missed when they first entered.

"Ladies, can I interest you in a raffle ticket or two?"

The voice sounded familiar to Holly, and she looked up to see her tablemate from last night seated behind a ticket table.

"Lydia," Holly exclaimed.
"Oh, my goodness," Lydia said. "Holly, right?"

"Yes ma'am," Holly replied.

"How wonderful to see you again," Lydia went on. "We are going to be raffling off a few items later if you'd like to purchase some tickets. We're raffling off four tickets to the *Hamilton* musical, and a Hamptons beach-house weekend. I believe the house has four bedrooms and sits directly on the water in Sag Harbor. I've also got my Hamptons home in the raffle, donating it to the lucky winner for a week. And there's dinner for two at Rao's, a pair of Yankees tickets, and breakfast for four at Tiffany's. Did you girls know that Tiffany's has reopened their Blue Box Café?"

"I did," Kirkland said.

Holly gestured to Kirkland. "Lydia, this is Kirkland. She's covering the Tulip Tea benefit for the *New York Times*."

"Lovely," Lydia said. "Tickets are five dollars each or twelve tickets for forty. That's a super deal and gives you more chances to win. The money from this event, the raffle, and the silent auction all benefit Bradley Banner's campaign. Great cause, as you know."

Holly and Kirkland looked at each other. Kirkland shrugged.

"I have a couple of twenties, I think," Kirkland announced. She looked at Holly. "Or if you have a twenty, we could each write our name on six of the tickets."

"Yeah," Holly said. "I've got some cash. But I actually left my purse down inside the larger bag I brought, which is at our table."

"Just pay me back after we're seated. No problem."

Kirkland looked through her bag, pulled out two twenties, and handed them to Lydia. Lydia pulled twelve tickets from her roll, tore them apart, and handed six each to the girls.

"Make sure to write your first and last names on the back along with your cell number," Lydia instructed.

Once they finished writing everything necessary on their raffle tickets, they placed them inside a large glass fishbowl on the table. Lydia was busy selling more tickets, so Holly and Kirkland walked into the other room and back to table twenty-eight. Two more women close to their age were seated at the table. "Hello," one of them said as they approached.

"I'm Faith. I'm with *The New Yorker*."

Then the other girl introduced herself.

"I'm Dakota, and I'm with the *Tawk of New Yawk.*" She said it with an amusing New York accent, and Holly couldn't help but giggle.

"It really is spelled the way I said it," Dakota assured her.

Once everyone had introduced themselves, the girls settled into their seats and made general comments about the table décor, the silent auction, and when the actual shindig would begin. Holly pulled her Canon from her large bag and snapped a few photos of the centerpieces.

"I think I will step outside for a moment," Holly told them. "I'd like to take some photos of that adorable custom-bar van with a few of the ladies standing near it."

The other girls nodded. "It is really cute. We took some photos of it when we arrived," Faith said.

15

Slay it, Girl

While she was taking photos near the entrance, Holly saw Garrison walk past. Her heart dropped a few feet. Her throat felt tight, and she coughed a little, trying to clear the feeling. She wondered if she should follow him and speak her mind. Or should she wait until she was about to leave? Neither seemed like the perfect time to call someone out on their unwanted behaviors. She turned back around and concentrated on the photos she was taking of a group of ladies holding their custom cocktails.

"Thank you," she told them.

She snapped the lens cap back on her Canon and was about to walk inside when Garrison tapped her on the shoulder.

"Holly," he said. "Bradley is almost here."

Holly nodded. "I . . ., um . . ."

Garrison interrupted with "She said you have something to present to her?"

"I do," Holly answered.

"Could you bring it to me after Bradley gets here? There's a small table that the table-top podium is sitting on. That's where I'm going to set a few things that will be presented to her. And I'll put your item on that table, next to the podium, before she's introduced."

A limo pulled up to the curb.

"She's here," Garrison said. He looked at Holly expectantly.

"Could you get it and meet me at the top of the stairs?" he asked. "I'm going to take Bradley upstairs to wait a few minutes. She might have a dress she wants to change into. Her entrance will be more dramatic if she descends the stairs when she enters the room."

"I'll go get it and meet you upstairs."

Holly went back to her table, set her camera down, dug through her large bag, and pulled out the thick plexiglass frame holding the mock-up of Bradley on the *Beyond* cover. Without a word to her tablemates, she went to the staircase in the hall and walked up. When she got upstairs, Garrison and the girl from the hostess stand were showing Bradley where she could change. Bradley had two other women with her, a smaller entourage for today.

Garrison came out of the room Bradley had gone into, closed the door behind him, and met Holly in the hallway.

"Here." She handed over the frame.

"Perfect," Garrison said. "There will be a time near the end of the program when the president of the Colony Club will speak and make a presentation to Bradley. Afterwards, she will introduce you. You'll come up, say a few words, and hand Bradley this frame. A few photos will be taken afterwards, then everything will wrap up. I think after all the speeches and presentations, they will announce the winners of the silent auction. There should be an agenda at each table, so you can follow along."

"Okay. I'll look for that."

Garrison turned away from Holly and toward the room Bradley had gone into, waiting for her to appear.

"Garrison," Holly said. "About what happened last night . . ."

He turned back to Holly, their eyes met, and he shook his head.

"Nothing to worry about," he said.

Holly stepped in close. It was not the perfect time to say what she wanted to say, but at that very moment, she felt bold. "There is something that does worry me," she said. Her voice sounded quiet and composed, but stern. "I didn't like the way you forced yourself on me without asking. That type of behavior is not okay. You groped me like some high school boy trying to go all the way in the back seat of a car. I was shocked by your behavior. It was like a caveman, and you should evolve from that already. In the future, you should be more thoughtful and considerate. Your actions have consequences. I'm not kidding. This is serious and something I feel strongly about and felt you needed to hear. Because I'd think a guy like you, or at least like the guy I thought you were, would *always* behave like a gentleman. There is no excuse to be anything but. To say, I was disappointed in the way last night ended is an understatement."

Garrison stared at Holly with a look of shock, then a sour look contorted his expression.

"She's ready," one of Bradley's crew said from the doorway.

They both looked in that direction, then Holly turned away from Garrison and went down the stairs and back to her table. Her heart was pounding, and a nervous sweat had broken out across her skin. But when she got to her table, she took a deep cleansing breath. She'd said what she needed to; it was done. By this time, most everyone was seated; only a few groups of ladies were still standing around talking. Holly found the agenda and picked it up to read. Dakota, who was sitting on one side of her, pulled her napkin from where it was lying across her plate to find her own agenda underneath.

"Oh, look," Dakota said. "There was an agenda under my napkin. We each have one. I guess we don't have to keep guessing what's going to happen after all."

The others giggled.

Waiters came around and filled everyone's glasses with their choice of still or sparkling water. Lydia walked through the room and up to the front, where she stopped at a small table. A table-top-style podium sat atop a round table that was covered in a white cloth. In front of the podium, a large blue and white teapot graced the center of the table. A tall bouquet of yellow tulips popped out from the teapot along with sprigs of English ivy that trailed down the sides of the teapot and curled along the front edge of the table. Lydia checked to see if the microphone was on, then she welcomed everyone to the Tulip Tea.

Lydia then announced they would start by giving away the raffle items. A lady wearing a large red hat and a long, flowing floral maxi dress walked toward the podium carrying the fishbowl with the raffle tickets. She stood next to Lydia. Then Garrison walked up and set the framed cover of *Beyond* face-down on one side of the table. He moved away as quickly as he'd approached, and the lady in red leaned into the microphone.

"First," the lady said, "we will be giving away four tickets to Tiffany's Blue Box Café. Her hand slipped into the bowl; she mixed the tickets a few times then chose one. She announced the winner's name. Applause and excitement danced through the air. Next, she announced the Yankees-tickets winner then the winner of the Sag-Harbor-house vacation. Kirkland won the *Hamilton* tickets, and she was beside herself. The winner of the dinner for two at Rao's was announced, and finally it was time to choose the winner of the last raffle item.

"And the winner of the week-long vacation at the house in Montauk goes to. . ." The lady dug around for a few seconds, then pulled out a ticket and read the name.

"Holly Curtis."

"What?" Holly said.

The others at her table clapped and cheered. Holly stood and walked to the front to receive whatever card or information she'd be given. Lydia handed an envelope to her.

"All of the information is in here," Lydia told her. "Including photos, my contact information, and everything you need to know. All you have to do is pick the week you want to come, and I'll make sure everything is set."

She winked at Holly, and Holly took the envelope from her.

"This is amazing," Holly said. "Thank you so much."

As Holly made her way back to her seat, the other lady moved to sit at a table near the podium while Lydia gave a passionate introduction of Bradley Banner. Holly got her camera ready and turned around in her seat in order to capture the moment as Bradley descended the stairs and elegantly made her entrance in a pale peach suit-dress. A thick mass of layered pearls graced her neckline, and she wore a large light-peach-colored hat. On her feet were nude glossy Christian Louboutin stilettos. Holly could see the signature red-soles each time Bradley took a step down the stairs. Holly and the others at her table stood in order to get better photos.

Once Bradley was at the podium, they snapped a few more shots, then put their cameras away. Holly opened the memo-recording app on her phone and turned it on to capture Bradley's speech. Although her talk was similar to the one she'd given last night, she added some specifics that were geared toward the women she was addressing today.

"Feminism by definition is simply the belief that men and women should have equal rights and opportunities." Bradley spoke slowly and gracefully. "It does not mean that women are men-haters, and it does not mean that women are mean or bossy. It is simply a belief in bestowing women with the right to earn the same salaries and job titles as their male counterparts. We know and we believe that we should have the same expectations for women as we do of men. We understand that women can achieve the same goals as their male counterparts and should be appreciated as much as men are. Growing up female in this country has its privileges. One of those is an equal-opportunity education. In some countries around the world, girls are not educated. Some of these countries might never let girls set foot in a classroom, while girls may end their education at the time of puberty, simply because around that time—or soon after—they will be expected to marry and bear children. In the eyes of their country, an education shouldn't be wasted on a woman."

Bradley paused, glanced around at the crowd, then finished her speech.

"There is a book I read several years ago that was a gift from an older woman in my life who at the time was like a mentor to me. The book was written by Melinda Gates, and it is called *The Moment of Lift: How Empowering Women Changes the World.* It's basically a memoir by Melinda about the Bill and Melinda Gates Foundation—which, by the way, is one of the largest charitable organizations in the world. And not only is it a memoir, but Melinda interweaves personal stories and data as she describes her twenty years of philanthropic work. During her advocacy, she realized that empowering women would require a comprehensive approach. It would require cultural awareness, along with everything from delivering tools to people to listening to what they have to say, and gently questioning their ineffective practices. It would require seeking help from community members, such as yourselves, and providing lifesaving information to those who desperately need it. Melinda saw the importance of sharing with them the benefits of contraceptives, which can combat poverty, improve women's health, and lower childhood mortality rates.

Silence had fallen around the room as all were held captive by Bradley's speech.

"Melinda's book explains the importance of education," she continued. "Keeping girls in school will lead to higher literacy rates and income growth. Helping to educate women from these third-world countries will curb premarital sex and early marriages. Well-educated women have healthier babies. Education increases their self-confidence and fuels their advancement. And, most importantly, her book emphasizes connection. People within the margins must be uplifted, and as women we must work together to demand equality. These are things that I truly believe are important in helping girls throughout the burrows of New York who could fall through the cracks without strong mentors, a good education, self-confidence, and the ability to continue their education past high school."

Bradley gave the audience a broad smile. "Women supporting other women. I have certainly felt your support today. So partner with me." She took a breath and with a strong, loud voice continued. "And when I win the election as governor, together we can make a difference; together we can make changes happen."

Applause broke out. Bradley waited a moment.

"Ladies, after leaving here today, make a choice," she continued. "Decide to use what you've been given. Use your personality, use your talents—either administrative or artistic, use your finances, and open your heart to serve that which is greater than yourself. And then you will have become truly empowered."

With affirming cheers and some tears on the attendees' cheeks, everyone in the room stood, clapping loudly. Lydia approached the podium and placed a hand on Bradley's shoulder. The two women embraced. Slowly everyone began to take their seats again. Waiters came around to each table and placed tea trays filled with the most incredible-looking fruits, desserts, small bites, and scones. More waiters added teapots filled with hot water and boxes full of tea bags to each table.

"Bradley," Lydia began, "it is my great honor to inform you that our membership of the Colony Club has voted unanimously to make you an honorary member with full benefits. Welcome to the oldest women-only social club in the city of New York."

Lydia took a gold sparkling pin from a box, leaned in, and pinned it near Bradley's left shoulder. Holly and the others at her table stood and snapped photos.

"Thank you," Bradley said. "Thank you all so much. I'm grateful."

"We will have you attend a special induction ceremony later," Lydia said to Bradley, then she read from a note she held in her hand. "Now, for another special presentation, I'd like to call on Holly Curtis to come up. Holly is a journalist and a writer for *Beyond* magazine, based in Atlanta. And as Holly makes her way to the podium, waiters are coming around with your tea selections and tea trays. Please enjoy these marvelous selections. And don't forget to make your final bids for the silent auction. We'll allow another thirty minutes before it closes."

By the time Lydia had finished her announcements, Holly had made her way to the front. Lydia moved to sit back at the table nearest the podium. Holly had only planned to say a few words and had not written a speech.

Holly greeted Bradley then turned to her audience. "Good afternoon," she began. "It is a privilege to write for *Beyond*, which, as some might know, is a magazine that features only women as its subjects. Female entrepreneurs, women-owned businesses, female authors, female musicians, and women in politics. The founder of *Beyond* is a young woman named Marla Monroe. It was Marla's goal to create a magazine that empowers women and recognizes them for who they are, what they've accomplished, and what they plan to accomplish in the future. Although *Beyond's* blogs are updated daily, our hard-copy issues are released in the fall and the summer. And our summer issue cover and cover story will feature Ms. Bradley Banner."

Holly picked up the frame from the table and held it up so that everyone could see it. More applause. She could see the girls from her table snapping photos with their cameras and their phones. Holly turned to Bradley and held the frame out for her to take.

"Ms. Banner, it's so great to be able to present you with this framed cover."

Bradley smiled at Holly, took the frame from her, looked at the cover, then said,

"Again, it's such an honor to receive this kind of recognition. Thank you, Holly, and thank you as well to your staff at *Beyond*. I'm thrilled and excited to be on the cover and to be the featured story. I'm grateful to everyone here today from the Colony Club. Thank you from the bottom of my heart for your support of me in the race for governor and for raising funds today through this incredible benefit. It fills me with so much joy and so much hope for a victory. Together, let's do this!"

16

Home Is Where the Heart Is

The girls at table twenty-eight enjoyed their tea sandwiches and scones. Holly held her teacup up and proposed a toast to the best young female writers at the Tulip Tea. They giggled and clinked their teacups together, knowing they *were* the only writers covering the tea. They challenged each other on who would end up with the best photos from the event. And they exchanged Instagrams and said they'd keep in touch. Then with the silent auction winners having been announced, things started to wrap up.

Bradley Banner had been going from table to table introducing herself and taking photos with all of the ladies as she'd done last night. But there would be at least three tables to go to before she'd get to Holly's, and Holly needed to get to the airport. She looked at her phone; it was almost five thirty. She shot a quick text to Bree asking her how long it would take to get to the airport, reminding her that her plane was leaving around nine. Bree texted back that it would take just over an hour, but that would also depend on traffic. Holly shot her a reply.

The event is basically over, and I can leave as soon as you get here. It's getting close to 5:30 and I'd rather be early to the airport than late.

Sure, no problem. I'm heading back over now. Be there in about 15.

Faith asked a lady sitting at the table next to theirs if she would take a group photo. Holly and Kirkland moved to stand behind Dakota and Faith, and a few photos were snapped with Faith's phone.

"I'll text them to you guys," Faith said.

"It was so nice to meet each of you," Holly said. "My ride to the airport is on her way. I'm going to wait outside."

The girls took turns giving Holly hugs and saying goodbye.

Kirkland smiled, took a step back, and did a sideways shimmy with her shoulders. "Have fun in the Hamptons," she said, throwing two pointed fingers in Holly's direction.

"Absolutely," Holly said. "Don't know when I'll get to go. But I've had a great time these last twenty-four hours in New York, and I'm glad to have met you guys. Have a great weekend."

Holly picked up her bag. As she walked past the table next to hers, Bradley was coming her way.

"Ms. Banner," Holly said, "it will be such an honor to write about you for the cover story. If I have any other questions, could I email those to you?"

Bradley nodded. "Yes. Do you want to write down my email?"

Holly pulled her phone from her bag and said, "Ready."

Bradley gave her the email address of someone who worked for her campaign, and Holly thanked her again before she made her way outside to wait for her ride. Within a few minutes, Bree arrived and drove Holly to the airport.

* * * * * *

She got to the airport fairly early, giving her enough time to change into comfortable clothes and shoes and to look through and edit photos from the weekend. She thought about Garrison and the way he'd just looked at her with a sense of shock and entitlement after she had confronted him on his appalling behavior. If she never heard from him again, it was fine. So much for her own small-town Hallmark love story.

The gate announcer's voice came over the loudspeaker, and all thoughts of Garrison vanished. Since this flight was also full, all passengers willing to check a bag would be allowed to board early. *What the heck*, she thought, and walked over to the desk and offered her bag to be checked. After all, she was headed home. And she wasn't interested in being held hostage again in the small, cramped area of doom in the back of the plane while a flight attendant tried to check last-minute bags using cocktail napkins.

Soon it was time to board. Holly had a window seat this time, and once the plane was in the air, she opened her tray table, took out her notebook, put in her AirPods, and began to jot notes while listening to the recording of her interview. Before she knew it, the plane had started its descent into Hartsfield-Jackson Atlanta International Airport. As soon as they landed, she texted Lofton to make sure she was on her way to pick her up. By the time Holly had gotten her bag—which, thank God, had not gotten stuck on the carousel this time—Lofton had texted that she was on her way.

Holly texted back to ask where she wanted to meet. Lofton said she had arrived and gave her the level and row where she was waiting in short-term parking. When Holly got to the spot, she looked around for Lofton's car. When she spotted it, she saw Lofton standing in front of her car next to a pilot. He held his pilot's hat under one arm, and his black suitcase sat next to him. He was an older gentleman who, in the darkness of the parking garage with only dim lighting, looked almost old enough to be Lofton's father. When they turned to face each other, they became silhouettes in the darkness, but Holly could see clearly that Lofton and this pilot were sharing a steamy kiss. When they pulled away from each other, Lofton grabbed his hand and pulled him back to her for another kiss.

She could see Lofton say, "I love you." Holly was still too far away to actually hear the words, but it was obvious that's what Lofton had said. The pilot did not say the same words back. He just took his bag by the handle and wheeled it toward the elevator.

This was news to Holly. Lofton had not told her she was dating a pilot or someone she'd met at work, or anything about this new guy in her life. Holly was curious, maybe even wary, about this man. He was older, and Lofton was only twenty-five.

Now that the pilot had moved on, Lofton was getting back into the driver's seat of her car, and Holly started walking toward her. She hoped Lofton would clue her in about her new love.

"Hey, girl," Holly said, walking up to the car.

"Hey," Lofton said. "Do you want to put your bags in the trunk?"

"Okay," Holly said.

Lofton popped the trunk so Holly could put her things inside, then Holly got into the passenger seat.

"Thanks for picking me up. I know it's a drag to come to the airport, especially at midnight."

Lofton smiled. "No problem at all. I was glad to do it."

Holly thought this would be the perfect time for Lofton to insert information about her beau. Holly waited for it to come, but it didn't. Lofton fiddled with the radio station and then picked up a pass card that let her through the exit without having to stop to pay.

"Anything new?" Holly asked.

"Nah," Lofton said. "Thank you so much for taking care of Padre. I know I've been gone longer than usual. In fact, I have a new, better schedule. I'm going to Greece next week."

"Wow. Fabulous."

"But let's talk about New York. How was it?"

"Well, I ran into an old crush from high school. He's actually Marla's New York contact, and he was filling in for Bradley Banner's PR person for the weekend. He owns his own PR company in the city."

"Oooh! This sounds like it's going to be good."

Mmm, Holly thought. *Not as good as whatever the story is behind your kiss with the pilot.* Holly told Lofton how good Garrison looked, how cool his job seemed to be, and what the first night's dinner was like. She even talked a little about going with him to Magic Hour. She left out that her night with him ended in complete horror. She feigned sleep deprivation and told Lofton she would finish the story later. She knew it would take a lot to conjure up the energy to talk about the subject.

"We could go out tomorrow night to celebrate your new success," Lofton said. "I don't leave for Greece until Monday. And you could finish your story about you and Garrison."

"Actually, I have to leave first thing in the morning to drive to Athens for my cousin's last theater performance. She's moving to London for six months. She's got enough credits to graduate, and since she got this internship in England, she's leaving in a few days. So there are parties for her and stuff, kinda like a graduation celebration. There's one tomorrow afternoon at the house she shares with her roommates. It's for her and her friends, then there's another one on Sunday afternoon at my parents' house. They've been planned for a while. Mom wanted me to be there, like, all day today to help set up stuff at home. It's going to be a crazy weekend with Denim's stuff in Athens then a family party at my parent's house. She's leaving on Monday for London, and I'm looking forward to spending time with her. And, I have to submit at least a rough draft of my cover story on Bradley Banner to Marla by Sunday. I know she'll want that as soon as I can get it to her."

"Shit, girl. Wow. That's really extra."

"I just wanna crash for a few hours before I have to repack and drive an hour and a half in the morning. Her party starts at one. Her performance is at five. Then I know Mom will have more for me to do on Sunday for the big pre-grad party-brunch thing."

"For real. I get it. I would not want to be you right now."

Holly leaned her head back onto the headrest and closed her eyes. After they pulled into their apartment complex parking deck, Holly dragged her bags from the trunk of the car, and the roommates walked silently up the stairs and inside. Padre greeted them at the door with a loud meow, probably grateful his two favorite people were home.

"Good night," Holly said, then went into her room and shut the door.

17

Barking Bulldawgs

Holly had set her alarm to get up by eight so she could take a shower and dry her hair. She put on a red dress and a pair of black chunky-heeled sandals in honor of her cousin's school, which was also her own alma mater—red and black for the University of Georgia Bulldogs. She pulled from her closet a few more dresses and tossed them into her carry-on bag from New York without unpacking anything. *I can do laundry at my parent's house if I need to,* she decided.

She walked into the main room of the apartment, which was a combination living/dining area that was open to the kitchen. Lofton was sitting on a barstool at the kitchen counter eating a bowl of cereal and talking to someone on the phone. She was giddy and giggly and was talking in quiet whispers. *Is that the pilot?* Holly wondered. She walked to the refrigerator and poured a glass of juice.

When Lofton saw Holly, she quickly told the person on the other end she had to go. Holly heard,

"I'll talk to you later, babe. My roommate is about to leave."

Lofton set her phone on the counter. "Heading out?"

"Yeah. I think I'll be home Sunday night but not sure. I guess it depends on how things go. How about you? When are you and your flight crew leaving for Greece?"

"It's Monday morning just before noon. I hate that we keep passing each other. But I'm really glad I have this new schedule with European flights now. I'm having a blast seeing new places."

"Wow. Cool. I hate that we keep missing each other too. Hopefully we can catch up soon."

Holly wondered if Lofton's new flight-attendant schedule had anything to do with her special pilot friend. She walked over to Lofton, and the two girls hugged each other. Padre jumped up on the counter next to them and headbutted Holly in the arm.

"I'll see you later, boy," Holly said. "Well, I need to get on the road. My mom is probably wondering what's taking me so long. Wish me luck."

"Have fun." Lofton called out over her shoulder.

* * * * * *

Holly pulled up in front of her cousin's house. Denim shared a house with five other girls who also went to UGA, all of them seniors. All of them would graduate in about a month, but Denim wouldn't walk in a graduation ceremony until she was back home in December. That's part of what made this day so special. At least for a day, Denim would get to do all the graduation celebrating she wanted with her friends.

A large white king-sized sheet was hanging from the top of the porch. It had been painted with scenes from London. In the upper right corner was Tower Bridge, the bottom corner featured Big Ben, and the other side had theater masks. There were two crying masks instead of the usual picture in which one was frowning and one was laughing. And painted at the bottom of the other corner was a crown. Across the top were the words: *Have the Thames of Your Life in London. We'll miss you, Denim.*

Holly left her suitcase in the car and walked up the steps to the front door. It all seemed too quiet for a party to be taking place in about an hour. After she stepped inside, she smelled the distinct aroma of cherry pie baking. And she heard voices coming from the kitchen, which was in the back right corner of the old house. There she found her mother and her mother's sister, her Aunt Joanne, busy stirring and prepping food. When a timer buzzed, Holly's mother turned around and pulled something out of the oven. Both Holly's mother and her aunt looked frazzled, and with the jumble of pots and pans made it look like they'd been baking for hours. Neither had noticed Holly was standing at the edge of the kitchen watching them work.

"Wow, this looks amazing, Mom."

"Holly! Thank God you're finally here," her mother said.

Holly walked around the large center island and gave her mother a side hug. Her Aunt Joanne, Denim's mother, came over to hug Holly as well. She kissed her on the cheek, then said,

"There's so much to do. Can you put the roses that are lying on the dining table in some water?"

"Sure," Holly said. "But where is everyone?"

Her mom continued to add ingredients to a dish she was preparing. "Dad and your brother have gone to pick up the Mexican food and the wings. They had to go to two different places. Denim wanted wings for the guys, and everyone else wanted Mexican. Oh, and I told them to pick up a couple of bags of ice. They left almost an hour ago."

"Where's Denim? And all of her roommates?"

Her Aunt Joanne answered. "Their caps and gowns arrived a few days ago. The girls have gone to take graduation pictures wearing those at a few locations around campus. I think they were doing some at Sanford Stadium, the Arch, and the fountain and then finishing up at Denim's sorority house."

"We need to get the table set so we can start bringing these pies and cookies out there," Holly's mom said.

"I'm going, Mom, but y'all need to calm down. You guys are not preparing a meal for the president or heads of state, you know." Holly grinned and in a teasing tone, said, "Or are you guys really filming a video to submit to the *British Baking Show*? Is this what this is?"

Holly laughed at her own joke. Aunt Joanne smiled, but her mom didn't look amused and just shook her head and continued working.

Holly walked into the dining room and saw that there was a red and white checkered tablecloth on the long table. Six bunches of red-rose bouquets lay in a pile on the table, and scattered around them were vases of all shapes and sizes. Holly went and found a pair of scissors, then filled each vase about half full with water. She trimmed the stems then added roses to each vase. She left the two largest arrangements in the center of the table and placed the smaller vases around the living room. As she was setting the last vase of roses down, she noticed a group of boys setting up folding tables and chairs in the front yard.

"Hey Mom," Holly called. "Some guys are here putting tables in the yard."

Holly's mom came rushing out of the kitchen carrying a pie wrapped in a dish towel.

"Denim and the girls said there will be a lot of people here today," she said, "and they wanted to make sure there was enough seating. I suppose most will sit in the living room on the couches, but she wanted tables and chairs too. Help me get all the desserts on the table. Your father and brother will be back soon with the food. I think we'll set the food on the kitchen island and put drinks and desserts on the dining table."

Holly helped her mom and aunt bring more of the delicious-smelling baked goods into the dining room. There were more pies—one apple, one peach, and one cherry—as well as a large tray of cookies. Her Aunt Joanne brought out a tiered tray of cupcakes. Then they assigned Holly to kitchen cleanup and dishwashing duty while her mother and aunt put out plates, napkins, drinks, and bottles of champagne. Soon her dad and brother were back with the food and bags of ice, and a buffet was set up on the kitchen island. More of Denim's friends showed up with more chairs for the front yard, and balloons were tied to the mailbox out front.

"When can we eat?" Holly's brother, Alex, asked.

"After everyone gets here," their mother answered. "I'm going upstairs to change. Keep an eye on your brother, Holly. In fact, tell him to move the chairs from the dining room into the living room for extra seating."

"I'm going to move the car," Holly's dad said. "I'm going to park it down the street in order to have more spots available near the house. I'll be back in a few."

Holly made a face, then looked at her younger brother, who was leaning against the counter with his nose inches above the food. "Get your face out of the food! Did you hear what Mom asked?" she snapped.

He backed away, hands up. "I was just smelling it. I promise I didn't lick anything." He was eighteen and a freshman at Georgia Southern, but most of the time, Holly thought he still acted like a high school freshman.

He walked up to Holly and pushed two fingers into her chest simultaneously. "Oops. Sorry," he said. "I didn't mean to push all of your buttons. I was looking for mute."

Holly rolled her eyes and pointed to the dining room. "Chairs," she said.

From the living room windows, Holly could see that more of Denim's friends had just arrived. They were putting tablecloths on the outdoor tables and placing "Go Dawgs" signs and other cute Georgia-Bulldog memorabilia in the center of each table. Holly decided to go out and see if she could help. Just as she stepped onto the porch, Denim pulled into the driveway, and she and her roommates got out of the car. They were wearing their graduation gowns over their dresses.

Holly ran over to Denim, and the two embraced, swaying together back and forth.

"I'm so glad you're here," Denim said. She looked at her friends and asked, "Y'all remember my cousin, Holly, right?"

The girls nodded and moved closer to say hello. One girl said, "I'm going to put this away as she slipped out of her graduation gown. Before she got to the stairs, one of the girls setting up centerpieces ran over to say hello to Denim and her roommates. Denim introduced her other friends to Holly.

"Nice to meet you guys," Holly said.

"Come on," Denim said. "Let's go up to my room so we can put these away." She held up her graduation cap, tassel swinging.

When they walked back inside, Holly's mom and aunt were filling a large drink container with ice. Her Dad was opening a bag of plastic cups and her brother was sitting on the couch looking at his phone. Denim's roommates had each gone into their rooms to put their things away, leaving Holly and Denim alone in Denim's room. Holly moved her mom's clothes from the bed and sat down.

"We have so much to catch up on," Denim said. She hung her graduation gown in the closet and placed her cap on the shelf. She turned back to face Holly. "Oh, my God, how was New York?"

"Good. A quick trip—only twenty-four hours. But a fun one too."

"After the show tonight, I'm planning to come back with you guys. Mom is staying overnight too. It's easier to get from y'all's house to the airport the next morning."

"Nice," Holly said.

Denim and Aunt Joanne were all that were left from her mom's side of the family. Denim's father had been killed in Iraq in 2007, right after Denim turned five. Holly's mom had really stepped up for her younger sister and her niece over the years, bringing them closer, and treating Denim as if she were her daughter, not just her niece. Their grandparents had passed away a few years later. The first to go had been their grandmother, who suffered from dementia, and a few years after that, their grandfather passed in his sleep from a heart attack.

Holly really felt as if Denim was her younger sister because they'd grown up together and spent summer vacations with each other. Holly had been a senior at UGA when Denim was a freshman, so they got to spend a little of their time in college together too. Today was a special day for Denim, and Holly was glad to be with her to celebrate her accomplishments and her upcoming theater internship in London, which was going to be amazing.

"Let's go downstairs. It's time to get our party on!" Denim said.

18

Celebrate Family

In the campus theater, Holly sat with her family on one side and Denim's roommates on her other. As the house lights dimmed and the atmosphere became shrouded in darkness, the opening act for Mozart's opera *Don Giovanni* came to life. Denim was playing the role of Donna Elvira, a woman who is seeking revenge after being scorned by the title character. The unfolding opera proved to be as much a comedy as it was a tragedy as Giovanni boldly continued to seduce every woman he encountered, leading more characters to go after him and even plot his death.

This was Holly's first opera, and she thought her cousin's performance was fantastic. Denim's family and friends were so proud of her; some of them even wondered how famous she might become in the future. After the curtain call, Denim's roommates headed back to their house to clean up from the earlier party, while Holly, her aunt, brother, and parents waited for Denim in the lobby, ready to whisk her away to her favorite local restaurant.

The group arrived at the Last Resort Grill, and the host sat their party of six at a table along an exposed-brick wall. Across from them, tall windows faced the busy street. Their host handed out menus and told them their server would be right with them.

"This place looks nice," Holly's mom commented.

"Mom, I think I brought you and Dad here at least once when I was a student," Holly said.

"Yes. I think I remember," Holly's dad replied. "Wasn't there a band playing? And they had cornhole set up outside on the patio?"

"Dad," Holly said. "That was parents' weekend at Live Wire for my sorority. We came here for lunch on a Sunday afternoon once."

Holly's dad nodded. "It's been a while since we've been in Athens," he said.

"It's Denim's favorite spot in town," Aunt Joanne said. "She always wants to come here when I visit. It's usually between this place and that little Café on Lumpkin."

"Love Café on Lumpkin," Holly added.

Denim smiled. "This place used to be a music club back in the sixties and seventies. A lot of famous people came through to play here. Acts like Jimmy Buffett and even Steve Martin. I love knowing the history behind places, you know?"

"I enjoy it too," Holly's mom added. "The history, I mean. And knowing who might have been in the same room years before me."

"Denim, your performance tonight was incredible. My first opera," Holly's dad said.

"I have an opera singer for a cousin," Holly said while doing a little wiggle dance in her seat.

"Will you always just do opera?" Alex asked.

"No. I eventually want to land a role in a Broadway musical. I'm hopeful my time in London performing at The Globe will give me the push and the opportunity to earn my chance in New York."

A server arrived to take their drink orders. Alex ordered an appetizer. Holly's dad ordered champagne for the table, telling the waitress they were celebrating his niece tonight, which Holly thought was such a dad move—to explain to the waitress what they were celebrating as if it was of any importance to her.

Holly's phone buzzed, and she saw it was Marla calling. She didn't want to seem rude, so she stood, saying she had to go to the restroom. As she walked away, she slid her finger across her phone to answer.

"Hey, Marla, what's up?"

There was loud music and talking in the background before she heard Marla say,

" Holly. Gary said everything went well in New York."

"Yeah." It was all Holly could get out before Marla continued.

"I have a feeling we should go ahead and share some photos on our socials to start promoting Bradley as our summer cover. Can you shoot me some photos? Have you finished editing those? Actually, I'm out tonight with Michael and some friends. Can you send them to Wagner? He's handling social media this weekend—Twitter and Instagram at least. I think if we can get some up on those platforms, we will get a ton of attention. I need a few more companies to pay for full-page ads for the summer issue before it's a wrap."

"Um, okay, sure. No problem, Marla. I'll work on getting some shots sent to Wagner tonight."

"Perfect. I knew you were the right person to send to New York. You are always professional. Always thinking about work, like a little mini-me. Gotta go. Oh, don't forget to send me a rough draft of your story tomorrow, please. Thanks, girl. Bye."

Marla hung up. Holly shook her head. *Wow.* She felt like she was in a tailspin. *Maybe I need some of Marla's Adderall.* She shook her head. *Definitely not.* Before she went back to the table, she quickly sent a text to Wagner.

Just got a call from Marla. She wants photos from New York of Bradley so we can post that she will be on our next cover. I'm at dinner with my family now but will get them to you soon.

Less than a minute later, Wagner responded.

Enjoy time with your family. Send pics when you can. Can't wait to hear about your trip.

When she got back to the table, her family was in the throes of laughter, reminiscing about one of their past vacations.

19
Burning the Midnight Oil

By the time Holly and Denim arrived at Holly's parents' home, it was after eleven. After dinner, the two of them had gone back to Denim's house to get her suitcases and computer bag, and to make sure Denim hadn't forgotten to pack anything. Holly had stood by and watched as her cousin held onto her roommates while they cried. There were tears of joy mixed with sadness and a longing for what would now be in the past—their college years.

Holly's parents' house hadn't really been her home since she'd moved away to start college seven years ago. Still, it always felt nice to be back. It was a comfortable feeling that Holly sometimes wished she could bottle up and pour out like a thick, fresh, floral-scented shampoo that would foam into the smoothest, richest lather. It was a feeling that instantly lifted her spirits, surrounding her with a warmth and comfort that could only come from walking into her childhood home and seeing her mother's eyes light up as she welcomed her with open arms. Tonight definitely felt like old times, since Denim had sometimes slept over before Holly left for college.

The two girls settled into Holly's old bedroom which still held remnants from her days gone by: her cheerleading photos, trophies, medals from competitions, and her favorite blanket, which was folded neatly at the foot of her bed.

Holly walked over to her desk, got out her computer and her camera, and plugged them both in. "I know it's eleven thirty, but I hope you don't mind," Holly said to Denim. "I've got some work to do tonight. I could do it downstairs though."

"No. Stay here, go right ahead. I'm just going to change into something comfortable and look through photos from today. And find some favorites to post."

Denim went into the adjacent bathroom to change while Holly pulled up all the photos from her New York trip. Carefully she looked through each, cropping some, and adding some highlights to others. After a while, she knew which ones she'd send to Wagner. They were the best images of Bradley. Two were during her speech at Sardi's, and the others were from the Tulip Tea. Kirkland had even texted her a candid of Holly with Bradley during the presentation of the cover mock-up. She emailed the selected photos to Wagner and Marla. Then she sent a quick text to Wagner letting him know he had the pictures.

Next, Holly decided to create an outline for her story. A few minutes later, Wagner responded.

Got it. Are you burning the midnight oil?

Ha. ha. It looks like you are too. I have a cover story to write. Surely you weren't waiting up for me to send you those pictures.

Maybe. Or maybe I just wanted to talk with you.

His response slightly stunned her. Denim came out of the bathroom, and Holly jumped.

"Sorry," Denim said. "Didn't mean to scare you. Did you forget I was here?" She giggled.

"Uh, no. My mind is just on other things, I guess."

"I'm going to get a glass of water. You want anything?" Denim asked.

"Thanks. I'm good."

Denim left the room, and Holly turned back to her notes, writing down a few questions that she wanted to email Bradley. Her phone dinged with another text from Wagner.

These are great photos, BTW. I won't post anything now since it's so late and not prime posting time for likes, follows, and all that Instagram algorithm stuff, ya know?

Before she could respond to the text, Denim returned, sneaking into the room with a hand over her mouth, a glass of water in the other, looking like she was trying not to be loud, or maybe she was holding in a cough.

"Have you seen what's in the dining room?" she asked with a squeal. The excitement in her voice was palpable.

"No. Why?"

"There's a giant carboard cutout of a red phone booth in there. Union-Jack banners, and a cardboard statue of a Royal Palace guard."

"A red phone booth and a Royal Palace guard? Oh, my gosh, Denim. I had no idea. Mom must have gone crazy with the decorations for the party tomorrow."

Thoughts of Holly's grad parties popped into her mind, and she remembered how often she had to reel her mom back in from some crazy party theme or idea that Holly just wasn't into.

"I am so sorry!" Holly said.

"Sorry? No. I love it."

Denim sat on Holly's bed and leaned back into the pillows. Holly joined her. Denim laid her head on Holly's shoulder. Holly's phone buzzed again. Seeing it was the same text from Wagner, she set her phone down next to her.

"I suppose our moms were in cahoots," Denim went on, "and they're having a ball planning these parties for me. I can't complain. I think Mom said she wanted to do an English-tea-party theme inside and a Georgia-Bulldogs-barbeque-cornhole type thing for the backyard. It should be a lot of fun."

"Do you know who's planning to come tomorrow?" Holly asked.

"My old theater coach from high school. My high school chorus teacher, some of our neighbors, and some friends from church. A few high school friends who are close enough to drive up, and two of my current—well, former—roommates are coming with a friend who couldn't be at the party yesterday."

Holly nodded. "I'll get up early and help Mom and Aunt Joanne so please feel free to sleep in."

Holly's phone buzzed again. It was another text from Wagner.

Good night, and good luck writing your cover story.

Denim must have seen who the text was from and asked, "Boyfriend?"

"Huh? Oh, the text? No, he's just a co-worker."

Denim gave Holly a 'can't-fool-me' look and said, "A co-worker who texts at midnight, gotcha."

Holly shook her head. "Seriously. He's in charge of social media for the magazine this weekend, and he needed photos from New York. I'd just texted him that I'd emailed him the pictures. That's all it was."

Denim shrugged. "Okay, so tell me about New York."

The two girls settled back into the pillows, and Holly told her all about the places she visited, the sights, the sounds, and the smells. She told her about the press dinner and the Tulip Tea benefit and running into her old high school crush. She told her how forward he'd been when he walked her to her room.

"I guess it's not in my future to have a Hallmark kind of heartwarming love story. More like a heartbreak-horror story. Anyway, the next day, I gave him the what's-what and told him exactly what I thought and that he should grow out of his entitled-caveman-asshole-type behavior. Because acting like a caveman is so . . . I don't know . . . last century."

Denim gave Holly a fist pump. "I'm glad you stood up to him, but, wow, Holly, how disappointing. I mean, to run into your old high school crush, have drinks with him, and even vibe with him, then he turns out to be a buttmuncher-fuck-boy. Girl, I'm glad you told him what you thought. What did he say after you gave him a piece of your mind?"

"Nothing. He looked at me weird is all. I mean, a sour look came across his face. I'll probably never hear from him again. But he's Marla's New York contact for events, PR, and stuff, so I don't know if I'll see him again or not. I actually hope I don't."

Denim nodded. "Do you think you should tell Marla?"

Holly let out a breath. "Honestly, I feel it was a personal interaction between me and a guy I liked from high school. He acted badly, but I seriously don't know if it's something I want to tell Marla about."

20

Party 2.0

The next morning, Holly woke early, went downstairs, and found her mom.

"Let me know what I can work on," she said.

Her mom took her into the dining room to show her the decorations. Just as Denim had said, there was a large cardboard cutout of a red phone booth, an English guard, lots of Union- Jack banners, and Union-Jack plates and napkins. Her mom and aunt could really use those if they were to ever gather the gumption to audition for that baking show they loved. Those props would be perfect. Holly thought about bringing that idea up until her mom broke the silence.

"Joanne and I will go to the store in a few minutes to get flowers and some last-minute items," Holly's mom told her. "In the garage are the Georgia Bulldog decorations. One is a giant blowup of Hairy Dog that Dad will need to plug in, and there are some UGA-themed cornhole games and a balloon display. I'm hoping your dad and your brother will work on setting that stuff up in the backyard if you don't mind setting up the English-tea-party theme in the dining room. I've left some china and teapots sitting on the table that can be part of the display."

Her mom pointed to the table. "You can use the white tablecloth that's there. And just pull out any crystal vases you can find for the flowers. Someone will be dropping off the custom cookies and cupcakes soon. Some of the cookies are London-themed; the others have UGA decorations. We'll use the UGA-themed cookies out on the patio."

Holly nodded. Her mom placed a hand on Holly's shoulder and gave it a squeeze.

"Thanks, sweetie," her mom said. "I'm going to make some cinnamon rolls and bacon for breakfast. Then Joanne and I need to get to the store to pick up last-minute food and drinks."

"Okay," Holly said. "And this party starts at three?"

Her mom nodded. "Yes," she answered, then went into the kitchen.

Holly got to work. She pulled out a chair to stand on, then hung the Union-Jack garlands from the ceiling. Then she set the plates out and gathered vases for flowers. After she placed the phone booth and the English guard in their spots, she snuck back upstairs to work on her cover story.

She checked for any new emails and saw that both Marla and Bradley's office had answered the emails she'd sent. Marla loved the photos, and Bradley's assistant had answered her questions for the article. She opened a blank Word doc and began writing. It was still early, and she hoped the sounds of typing wouldn't disturb Denim, who was still sleeping.

After an hour, Holly thought she had a good start to her story. She'd started to read over what she'd written when her phone began blowing up with Instagram notifications. She pulled up the app to take a look.

Wagner had just posted the photos from New York. First, she saw a close-up of the upcoming summer cover. She swiped left, and the next photo was the candid of her presenting the framed cover to Bradley. For the magazine's Instagram story, he'd used the photo of Bradley speaking at Sardis, and of course he'd tagged her in both the post and the IG story. He'd also added a "new-post" pic for the next Instagram story, just in case some saw the stories, but not the official page post. The caption for the post was cute. "Cover queen," it said, and it went on to talk about Bradley's campaign for governor. *Mmm. Good job, Wagner,* Holly thought. Then she went back to reading through what she'd written.

There are all sorts of feel-good stories out there about people making their way from poverty to power or moving from the wrong side of the tracks to the road to success. And we need those stories, because we need to learn about the heroes who took those paths and made the sacrifices that were needed. They're the ones who overcame the odds and can now talk about their achievements as superstars and shining examples. Our cover story and woman of the year, Bradley Banner's life is one filled with jubilation and triumph.

Banner's life began in rural eastern Kentucky. Her family didn't have a lot of financial resources, but that never stopped Banner from dreaming. She made sure she always got good grades, and one day she decided to try her luck in a pageant, and she won. The prize-package money allowed her to sign up for a more advanced pageant, and, again, she won. She didn't win every pageant after that, but she did get sponsorships and was able to hire a pageant coach.

After winning Miss Teen Kentucky, in high school, she was able to attend the University of Kentucky at no cost to her family, thanks to money she won in the pageant and to her great grades. Pageants had helped Banner find her style. They helped her to feel confident, speak eloquently in public, and ace in-person interviews. Most importantly, those competitions taught her how to get along with many personality types. Some might think that claims of success by way of the world of pageants sound like a joke from Hee Haw, *or something Honey*

Boo Boo would say. But for Bradley Banner, success was undeniable. And during college, she continued to climb the ladder of victory. This included winning elections in her sorority and, in her final year at university, the Miss Kentucky crown.

When her year as queen began, she toured the country for speaking engagements and other pageant events, promoting her philanthropy. Banner's chosen cause was securing help for underprivileged women and children in poverty-stricken areas of her home state. She became the spokesperson for the Christian Appalachian Project and soon was a nationally recognized personality. She was sought out by Victoria's Secret, and that relationship led Banner to a lucrative modeling career. This allowed her to continue to find ways to serve and volunteer with New York nonprofits. But what she wanted most was to use her voice full-time to help others, so after her modeling career ended, she started her own talk show, In A New York Minute. *Through her talk-show platform, she was able to bring in guests from nonprofits all around the world. She could host guests who wanted to speak out against violence, whether it was gender based, domestic, gun-related aggression, or bullying, Banner has raised awareness about many issues through her show.*

Banner knew she wanted to run for governor of New York after she'd—

Holly sprang almost to the ceiling when a pounding on the door startled her and woke Denim.

"You guys can't sleep all day when there's stuff to be done," Alex said through the door.

Holly got up, cracked the door open, and looked out at her brother.

"I was already up. Now you've woken Denim. What's your deal?"

"Dude. Dad's got me setting all this stuff up in the backyard. Why are you still in your room?"

"Why are you worried about it? Besides, I set up the dining room earlier this morning. You should probably get back to work."

Holly shut the door in Alex's face.

"I can't believe I slept so long," Denim said. "What time is it? I should be downstairs helping."

"It's just after eleven. Don't worry about it. There will be plenty of us working on setting up. I think our moms just got back from the store. Why don't you take a shower? I'll go down and see what I can help with. After you're done, come down and we'll switch places. And by all means, ignore Alex."

* * * * * *

Holly kept busy during the party refilling the punch bowl, throwing trash away, and taking photos of Denim and her guests. By seven that evening, the party had ended, everyone had gone, and the girls were sitting with their moms on the covered patio. Alex had left to head back to Georgia Southern, and Holly's dad was watching golf on TV.

"Aunt Jane," Denim said, "I can't thank you enough for everything you did to make this weekend so special." She looked at her mom. "And you too, Mom. And, Holly, thank you for being here. I know you have been going Mach 5 with your hair on fire in order to help with my celebration while also trying to write a cover story in order to get it turned in on time."

"Please," Holly said. "Don't even think about it. I wouldn't have missed this for the world."

"We were glad to do it, honey," Holly's mom said. "No need to thank us. We are so proud of you. And we are going to miss you."

"I hope you'll come to visit me in London." Denim looked at her aunt and her mom, and then at Holly.

"We've already been talking about a trip this summer," Holly's mom said.

"You won't be able to keep me away," Denim's mom added. "After you get settled, we'll find time to come sometime this summer."

"What about you, Holly?" Holly's mom asked.

"I don't know. You know how crazy my work is. I just never know when or for how long I can be gone. But the summer issue will release around the end of April, so I might have some free time around the first week of May. Speaking of which, I need to get back to my story. I've got to at least submit a rough draft to my editor before the day ends." Holly stood. "I'm going to go to my room and work for a bit. But I'll come back and help take down decorations."

"No," Holly's mom said. "Let's leave those. Your dad and I can get those put away later this week. Go do your thing. I'm pooped. I think I'll sit out here for a while. The weather's been really nice today."

"Same," Denim's mom said. "For the last Sunday in March, it's been very pleasant."

Holly watched as Denim curled up next to her mom, content to just be. Holly turned and walked inside, went up the stairs to her room, and sat at her desk, where she finished reading through her cover story.

Bradley Banner has proven herself successful in many endeavors. And if elected governor, she has plans to combat violence, enforce gun laws, and help New York's economy grow. And, most importantly, she is a strong advocate for women of all ages. She's got a proven track record in service and volunteering with many nonprofits. Her talk show not only airs top stories from the world of entertainment, ranging from the latest fashion trends to books and movies, but it also updates viewers on the latest news about politics, families in need, and nonprofits around the world working for the greater good. Banner has shown us how to love, serve, recognize needs, and help others as well as how to do it with grace and gratitude. She has also shown us that there's always room for growth. Our staff at Beyond is proud to honor Bradley Banner as Woman of the Year.

Holly looked at the clock in her room. *Not too bad on the timing,* she thought. *At least I'm not scurrying around trying to finish and send this at midnight. Maybe Marla will think it just needs a few tweaks. Who knows? If it's not good enough for the cover story, at least I tried.*

Just as she clicked "send" on the document, a text popped up. It was from Wagner.

How's our cover girl with the cover story? Everything going okay?

Just sent it to Marla to read. It's rough but she wanted a rough draft as soon as I had it. Wish me luck.

Did he just call me a cover girl?

21

Good Luck and Goodbyes

About an hour after Holly submitted her rough draft to Marla, she got an email from her. Marla made a few suggestions, nothing too major, and Holly was glad to make the corrections and go to work on a few rewrites. When she submitted the story for the second time, she asked Marla if she could be late to the office in the morning since she was still at her mom's house in Roswell. It was getting really late, and the drive to the office in the morning would take almost an hour. Staying where she was for the night would give her more time with her cousin and family. Marla emailed, Sure. See you later, and thanks for getting this to me. I know you've had a busy past few days.

After sending the corrected story, Holly thought about texting Wagner to tell him about it. Then she thought, *nah, he's probably not interested*. Denim came into Holly's room after spending quality time hanging out downstairs with her mom. She plopped down on the bed and said,

"I feel like my whole life is about to change."

"Yeah," Holly agreed.

Holly lay down on the bed next to Denim.

"Are you feeling a little scared?" she asked.

"I'm feeling a lot of things. Nervous, excited, anxious and afraid."

"Just keep reminding yourself how talented you are. Focus on the positives, especially when anxious thoughts creep into your mind. Start naming all the things you're grateful for. It's always worked for me. I feel better right away when I switch gears to think of all the great things in my life."

Denim smiled and looked at Holly. "You're right. That's good advice."

"I know there are so many things we have no control over, but what we think about and how thankful we are and how kind we are to others—those are all under our control. And knowing our moms, they'll both be praying for you every day. It's one thing I felt I could always rely on, my mom's prayers."

Denim nodded. "Yeah. Those are priceless."

Holly reached over and took one of Denim's hands in hers. She squeezed it tightly.

"It's getting late," Holly said. She got up and started moving around the room gathering things and packing.

"I've got to get up and drive to work in the morning," Holly said. "Although, I have permission to come in after nine, so I probably won't even leave here until then. I know you guys don't have to leave for the airport until almost four since you're flying to London on the red-eye, so I don't want to wake you."

Denim sat up crisscross on the bed. "Are you kidding? I'm not going to sleep through saying goodbye."

* * * * * *

Tears were shed the next morning during breakfast. Holly and her cousin shared a final hug, then Holly got into her car and headed into Atlanta to start a new week at work, hopefully a celebration week. She was on her way as the author of a cover story for Atlanta's trendiest women's magazine. She was feeling really good when she walked through the doors of Beyond. She held her head high; her spirits were even higher. She looked around but didn't see anyone at their desks. After opening her bag, she took her laptop out and set it on her desk. When she heard voices coming from the conference room, she headed that way.

Standing in the doorway, she could see Marla was conducting a meeting. The first person to notice Holly walk in was Wagner. He smiled at her, then everyone else's eyes landed on Holly too.

"Good morning," she said, but it came out sounding like a question.

"Oh, good. You're here," Marla said.

Holly walked over to an empty chair and sat between Kali and Stella. Stella shoulder-bumped her and gave her a sly-dog grin.

"Just to catch you up on what we were discussing," Marla began, "we were thanking Wagner for posting the photos about Bradley being on our summer cover. Since those posts went up on our Twitter." She shook her head. "X, I mean," Marla rolled her eyes in a way that seemed she was not only annoyed by forgetting the new name, but also in a way that would imply she thought the new name for Twitter was a little off. "and Instagram." She smiled broadly. "We've gotten three new full-page advertisements. And, yes, those companies have already paid for their ads. The summer issue is almost ready. And *thank you*, Holly, for taking the photos and putting together the cover story."

Holly nodded and looked over at Wagner, who was watching Marla like this was no big deal. But for Holly it felt huge. She had a real cover story. She was bursting at the seams with pride.

"You haven't really missed anything, Holly," Marla said. "We had just gotten the meeting started with the news about the ads right before you walked in."

"It's great news. "Congratulations," Holly said.

Wagner suddenly looked nervous. "Marla," he said, "I do need to point something out. This is not great news. It's not horrible, and it is something fixable, but it's a problem. Um, that is if it's not handled soon, maybe within the next few days."

Marla looked slightly annoyed. "What problem, Wagner?"

"We've run out of space in the cloud."

"The cloud?" Marla asked.

"Right," Wagner said. "Our space in the cloud is full."

"But it's, like, the cloud, right?" Marla said. She looked up, and her next question seemed to be directed at the ceiling. "How can the cloud be full?"

"The space that we paid for, the cloud space you bought from Apple when you started Beyond three years ago—it's full," Wagner said. "We need to discuss purchasing more space. There are lots of options. Businesses usually purchase their cloud space from Amazon, whereas some individuals purchase cloud space from Apple. But there are of course other options too. I think if we purchase three or four terabytes, we should be fine. Definitely not an external hard drive, though. If there was ever a fire everything would be lost."

Marla looked confused, Joe looked bored to tears, Kali was in a daze, and Stella was staring at Wagner. Holly was staring at him too but in a slightly different way. Hearing Wagner talk about nerdy, geeky software stuff was a real turn-on for her, but why was that? She had no clue. But, holy heck, she couldn't stop looking at him.

Today, Wagner's slim build was accented by a pinstriped navy and white button-down. He had the top two buttons undone. His curly brown hair was always slightly messy, and today it casually flopped a little bit over his left eye. Holly was a little jealous of his amazing eyebrows. His lips were plump, but not over-the-top large. His nose was a little long but thin, which made for a handsome profile with his sculpted jawline and high cheekbones. He had a smooth olive completion, a bit of a Mediterranean-look. If he had a pair of tortoiseshell glasses, he might even look a little like an Abercrombie model—very sophisticated. She wondered what he'd look like with his shirt off; would he have a hint of a six-pack?

"Holly!" Marla yelled.

Holly jumped and turned her attention to Marla.

"Have you fallen asleep sitting up?"

"Um, no. Sorry, Marla. I'm awake. My apologies."

"You wrote a heck of a cover story. We were just congratulating you is all."

"Thank you," Holly said, sounding meek.

As the meeting continued, Marla gave instructions for this week's social media. Stella listed topics that would be on the blog. Wagner mentioned the podcast guest for the week and said the Indigo Girls would be on next month. Kali gave updates on this week's photo-shoot locations. Then Marla said the summer issue would go into review on Wednesday, so everyone should be prepared to work on copy edits.

"Okay, everyone can head back to their desks and get to work," Marla announced. "Except, Holly, I need you, Joe, and Wagner to go over the photos for your cover story and hand-pick the ones you want, then get those suggestions to me later today. And, Wagner," Marla said, waving a finger between him and Holly. "you and Holly work together to pick some of Holly's photos from New York for the website."

Holly's heart beat fast; suddenly her palms were clammy. For some reason, the idea of being close to Wagner made her nervous. She nodded at Marla but couldn't bring herself to look at Wagner. Suddenly, someone with a deep voice called out from the lobby.

"Delivery."

"I'll get it," Kali announced.

Kali walked out of the conference room, followed by Marla, Joe, and Wagner. Stella turned to Holly and asked,

"You doin' okay? You seem off today. I know you are probably exhausted from New York and this weekend's parties and all. You should chill today. If you need me to write your blog, I will."

Holly smiled. She had been on top of the world when she walked into the office earlier, but somehow she'd gotten bamboozled with those sexy-time feelings for Wagner.

"It's crazy to say this, I know," Holly said, "but while Wagner was talking about how many terabytes of storage the company needed . . . I don't know. I drifted off into this lusty daydream and couldn't take my eyes off him."

Stella's eyes grew big. "Well, bite my terabutt," she said, but before she could continue her thought, Kali walked into the conference room with a large bouquet of yellow tulips.

"Someone must have a secret admirer," Kali said, then handed the bouquet to Holly.

22

If Tulips Could Talk

Holly looked at the tall bouquet of yellow tulips interspersed with long-stemmed green berries. She thought the flowers were probably from her parents to celebrate her first cover story. There had been so much celebration around Denim's graduation and move to London that Holly's milestone moment had not gotten much attention.

"Wowzah. Those are beautiful," Stella said. "There's a card. Let me hold the bouquet while you take it out and read it."

The three girls moved out of the conference room and into the open space of the main office. Wagner was hanging around close by. His hands were stuffed into the front pockets of his khakis, and he looked as if he were waiting on someone, which he kinda was. Joe had gone back to his desk, and Marla's office door was shut.

When Holly handed the bouquet to Stella, one of the accented Hypericum berries nestled throughout the tulips smacked Stella in the nose.

"Watch it," Stella said. "I don't want death by tulip to be the cause of my demise."

Kali waved her hands in excitement. "Hurry up," she said. "Let's see who they're from."

Holly opened the card and read the note silently. A look of dread and doom fell across her face. Her stomach dropped to her toes, her mouth went dry, and her throat felt tight. Sweat began to pool above her lip as anger started bubbling inside. She took a deep breath then told the girls,

"They're just from a friend," she lied. "Just wanting to say congrats on the story."

Quickly, she tucked the card back into its envelope and poked it onto its plastic stick within the arrangement.

"Cool," Kali said. "I'm going to take a look at the photos you took really quick and put in my two cents for whatever that's worth."

Kali walked past Wagner, who was still standing nearby. Holly heard her say, "You comin'?"

Still holding the bouquet, Stella leaned into Holly and whispered, "I know Wagner is waiting on you to choose the photos for the website, and you need to get to it, but I don't think these flowers were from a friend."

Holly shook her head. "No. They're from Garrison Simmons," she hissed. "The PR guy from New York. We went out, even made out. But he turned out to be a chauvinistic asshole. I didn't like how forward he was. I felt sexually assaulted." That came out much louder than she really wanted it to, and she wondered how much Wagner had heard. "If you're heading back to your desk, will you take the tulips and set them on mine?" She waved her hand flippantly. "I need to go."

Holly glanced at Wagner, who was looking at his phone. Was he waiting on her, or was he trying to listen in on her conversation about the flowers? She watched as he slowly walked toward his desk, which was next to Joe's.

143

"You need to tell me about this guy later," Stella said. "I want to know more about what happened with you and him. And we should definitely discuss telling Marla about it."

"Shhhhhh!" Holly said, giving a warning look to Stella before walking away. She turned back around to see Stella walking toward her desk with the giant bouquet of yellow tulips in hand.

When Holly got to Wagner and Joe's workstation, Kali was pointing to the screen, showing Joe her favorite photos of Bradley. Wagner turned away from the computer to look at Holly.

"It's not your birthday, is it?" he asked with a glowing smile.

Wagner's smile made Holly feel calmer. "No, not my birthday," she answered. "Just flowers from an old friend." She returned the smile.

"Let me pull up another chair for you," Wagner said, walking away to get one of the chairs that sat against the wall outside of Marla's office.

When he came back with the chair, Kali had started to gather her things for her next photo shoot. "I'm off to the 'hole-in-the-wall selfie museum,' Kali said. "It's donut themed, get it?" she said with a laugh.

"Sounds fun," Holly threw out. As she took her seat, her hand brushed the top of Wagner's, and a tingle of desire shot through her, which almost made her gasp out loud. She cleared her throat and tried to shake the feeling.

Wagner stood over her shoulder while Joe, seated next to Holly, pulled up the photos one by one. They began to rank and sort them for the cover story, website, or social-media posts with some earmarked for more than one category. A few minutes into the search for the best photos, Wagner moved a chair next to Holly's and sat down. Every once in a while, when he pointed to a photo, the sleeve of his shirt would skim across her arm, and she would catch a whiff of his woodsy, tobacco-scented cologne. After forty-five minutes they had their selections.

"Thanks, guys," Holly said. She started to stand.

Wagner moved her chair back for her.

"I'll get these ready for the summer issue," Joe said. "Marla wants to go over the layout in tomorrow morning's meeting. Copy edits will begin on Wednesday, and I think we have to have everything ready for print on the tenth. The magazine will hit newsstands across the Southeast—and a few big outlets in and around New York City—on the twenty-seventh."

"Thanks, Joe," Holly said. She turned to walk away.

"Uh, Holly," Wagner said, snagging her attention. "It's almost April first," he said with a shy smile. "I should get my best jokes together."

"Yeah," Holly said. She stopped walking and turned back to face him. "I guess we could add 'Best April Fools' Jokes' to one of the blogs that day. You know any really funny ones? Or are you going to save the best ones for us?" Her voice simmered with tease. "Maybe shock everyone in the office, who, will, of course, have forgotten it's April Fools' Day?"

Wagner stepped closer to Holly. "Remember the episode of *The Office* when Jim put Dwight's stapler in Jell-O?"

They both laughed. "Love that show," Holly said. Her eyes held his gaze for a beat, then she said, "I need to get to work on today's blog post. And you probably need to go back to saving us from getting lost in the cloud or whatever." She giggled. "Talk to you later, Wagner."

"It's saving space in the cloud so we don't lose anything important," he said.

She waved her hand above her head but kept walking toward her desk, where the tulips were front and center. Stella wheeled around in her chair to face Holly with a look of expectation on her face.

"Spill the tea, girly," Stella said.

Holly sat at her desk and turned her chair toward Stella. "You know how I went to Magic Hour after the press dinner party at Sardi's?"

Stella nodded. "Yep."

Holly ran her tongue over her lips, took a breath, and crossed her arms before she said, "Garrison Simmons is my old high-school crush."

Stella let out a loud gasp. "No f'ing way."

Holly smirked and rolled her eyes. "Yes, way. We recognized each other at Sardi's during the press dinner. He spoke to me, and he had been the one to make my reservation at a rooftop bar since those can be hard to get. He asked if he could join me, and I was thrilled. It was like I was living out some gushy romantic-movie fantasy. We were having a great time, but then things got a little steamy, and he got too handsy. Like really, really handsy. It scared me a little. When we were saying goodnight later at the door to my room, he got that way again, and I was honestly afraid the guy would bust his way into my room and . . ."

She trailed off, but Stella got the picture.

"Oh, my gosh, Holly. What did you do next?"

"When an older couple walked by, I pushed past him, slipped into my room, shut the door fast, and pulled out the extra lock. Then I watched through the peephole until I thought he had left. The next day I gave him a piece of my mind."

"And what did he say?"

"Nothing. He looked at me weirdly. I didn't think I'd hear from him again. I certainly was not expecting this." She pointed to the tulips.

Both girls looked at the arrangement on Holly's desk.

"Those *are* gorgeous, though. But now they are giving off a creepy vibe," Stella said. "What does the card say?"

Holly plucked the card from its plastic holder, opened it, and read it aloud to Stella.

"'Holly, it was great to see you. I had fun the other night, and I want to say I'm sorry for any misunderstanding. Can I call you? I hope we can clear things up, maybe start over.' And it's signed Garrison Simmons."

"Hmm," Stella said. "Sounds like he's trying to do the right thing."

That made Holly laugh. "I think that time might have passed. Even if he sent me flowers and nice cards every day for a month while begging my forgiveness, I don't think I would accept the apology." She shrugged.

"What are you going to do? Will you call him?"

"I don't know. He's following me on Instagram. But maybe if I ignore him, he'll go away. After all, he's thousands of miles away. He'll eventually give up, I suppose. I just don't want him to get the impression that I'm still into him. His forward behavior was definitely a turn-off; it was sexual assault. Maybe he's used to dating girls who like that stuff on a first date. But it wasn't even a date. I mean, I know we had known each other in high school, and he'd been my secret crush, but it wasn't like we were dating. We were just hanging out, catching up on old times. Maybe some kissing was involved—or a lot actually—before he took things too far. But he had no reason to assume, you know?" She paused and rolled her eyes. "Forcing himself on me like some sex-crazed maniac."

Holly's phone dinged with a text from Wagner. She picked up her phone to read it, and a huge smile broke across her lips. She brought her fingers to her mouth as she read the text again.

Did you hear the one about the guy who swapped the labels on the pumps at the gas station? It was an April Fuel's joke.

Stella looked at Holly's phone and saw the text was from Wagner, then she looked at Holly.

Stella steepled her fingers and tapped them together like Gru from the Minions movie. "Something else is going on, and you've got more tea to spill," she said.

23

My Trivia Team Thinks I'm Smart

The next morning Holly arrived at work on time, and Wagner was waiting for her as she walked into the office. He'd even texted her earlier to say he'd have coffee made and she didn't need to worry about making a cup before she left home.

"Good morning," he said, then handed her a cup with steam wafting from the top. "I put two pumps of vanilla in it and some oat milk."

"Wow. Okay. Thanks, Wagner." Holly took the coffee from him, and they walked further into the office.

"I guess I've been paying attention to details over the past year and a half," he said.

Holly nodded. "I guess so. I had no idea I'd announced my coffee preferences so often. But maybe I have."

Wagner smiled then asked, "Why was everyone so tired on April first?"

Holly shrugged. "Why?"

"They'd just finished a long thirty-one-day March."

Holly spit some of her coffee out. When a broad smile appeared on her face, Wagner seemed glad that he was amusing Holly and added another corny joke. "What monster plays the most April Fools' jokes?"

"I don't know. Which one?" Holly asked in a singsong voice.

"Prankenstein."

Holly snorted and rolled her eyes. "Good one. Thanks for the coffee, Wagner."

They parted ways as Holly walked to her desk, where she saw Stella watching her.

"I never thought I'd see the day," Stella said, "when you arrive at the office looking all hot and bothered over bad dad jokes and giggling with the person you had thought was so nerdy—you'd never think to give him a chance."

"What? We're friends. He's nice."

Stella leaned closer to Holly. "Holly, after what you told me yesterday about your sexy daydreams during the office meeting, plus the way you practically swooned over one of his corny jokes, I'm thinking you might need to change your panties."

Kali walked up. "Who needs to change their panties?"

"No one," Holly answered.

Stella pointed to Holly. "She lies. She's got an office crush on you-know-who."

"Nooooo," Kali said. Her eyes grew big. "Has our girl finally come around and embraced our love-sick office puppy's affections?"

Stella nodded. "Oh yes."

Holly looked flustered. "Stop, y'all," she insisted. "Nothing is going on."

"Not yet," Stella added.

"Mmm. Is he riding with us to trivia tonight?" Kali asked. She moved her shoulders and hands up and down like she was starting a TikTok dance.

Holly turned her computer on and started reading emails. "Crap," she spit out. "Now Garrison is emailing me to ask if I received the flowers." She glanced at the bright yellow tulips, which were looking larger than life on the corner of her desk.

Kali looked confused. "You said they were from a friend. Who's Garrison?"

Holly turned around to face Kali. "He was my crush in high school, who just happens to be Marla's PR contact in New York. We hung out a little after the press dinner last Thursday night, and he was. . . well, let's just say he was not a gentleman after he walked me to my door. I gave him my thoughts on that, after which he stared at me as if I had two heads. Now he's apparently had a change of heart and wants to apologize for his caveman-like behavior. You know, with the age-old I'll-send-flowers' routine."

Holly turned back to her computer and typed out a quick response to Garrison, letting him know point-blank that sending flowers would not sway her opinion of him or his behavior.

"Wow," Kali said. "When it rains, it pours. And right now, for you, my friend, it's raining men."

Holly turned away from her computer and spoke. "Wagner does not need to start riding to trivia with us. Who would Joe ride with? And, besides, we need to keep encouraging Marla to join us. We are team Beyond Amazing, of which she is a part, and she needs to take a break from working so hard. Don't you guys think so?"

"I know she works too hard," Kali agreed. "But just in case, Marla could ride with me and Stella, and you could ride with Joe and Wagner."

Holly rolled her eyes. Just then Marla came out of her office and called everyone into the conference room for the magazine-release meeting.

Everyone took their seats at the conference table. Marla busied herself plugging her laptop into the projector. Then she walked over and flipped off the lights. Stella leaned in and whispered in Holly's ear. "Don't do anything too crazy while the lights are out," she said with a grin.

"Really?" Holly said, deadpan, giving Stella a look.

"Okay," Marla said, gathering everyone's attention. "Here is the layout with ads and copy."

First a large image of *Beyond* with Bradley Banner on the cover was projected onto the conference room's whiteboard.

"Comments, suggestions?" Marla asked.

"Love it," Kali said. "I love how you chose the photo of her holding the framed mock cover. It's a cool shot."

Marla flipped to the next slide, which was the editor's page, where Marla published her thoughts and gave insights about the issue. She continued to go through the pages, asking for comments on the layout and the order of advertisements. Everyone seemed to be in agreement that the ordering of the pages looked good. There was some discussion about the last few pages, and once that was settled, Marla gave them their assignments for copy editing.

As the day went on, Holly looked forward to going to trivia with her office mates—and maybe even sitting next to Wagner.

* * * * * *

Later, when everyone but Marla was gathering their things to head out for dinner and team trivia, Holly encouraged Marla to join.

"One of these days I will, Holly. Thanks for the invite."

"I just worry you're working too much," Holly replied.

"And I appreciate your thoughts. Y'all have fun and win first place for me. Team Beyond Amazing can't always come in second. We have a famous model, talk-show host, and hopefully New York's next governor on our cover. We should be unstoppable."

Holly snickered at that last comment. "Yep, definitely. Have a good evening, Marla."

Later at the restaurant, the office mates gathered at their usual table, then Kali went over to get their trivia answer sheets and scorecard. Wagner made sure to sit next to Holly. He leaned toward her and offered up another April Fools' joke. Wagner's focus was all on Holly when he asked, "April Fools' Day is the favorite holiday of which animal?"

Holly looked puzzled. "Don't know," she said.

"The silly goose," Wagner said.

Holly laughed. Joe let out a groan. "Dude, lame," Joe said. Wagner looked embarrassed. But when Holly said, "I think his jokes are kinda cute," Wagner perked up again, as if that was the one thing he needed to hear.

Darby stopped by their table to take their drink orders. "My friends and I loved how the 'All Things Taylor Swift' podcast episode turned out," she said. "Thanks again for having us on."

"No problem," Wagner offered. "Glad it worked out. It's been one of our more popular episodes. Thanks for sharing and tagging us on your Instagram."

"Anytime you want us to be on again, we're game." Darby looked directly at Wagner. "I know Jada especially had a good time."

Holly watched to see how Wagner would respond to Darby mentioning her flirtatious friend. He just smiled at her, then told her he wanted to order a Terrapin Golden Ale.

The trivia guy's voice came over the loudspeaker to give the rules and point values, then he announced the categories for the first round. "Tonight, we will start out with fashion, animals, music, and history. Remember you can only use a point value once, so use your higher numbers for the answers you are sure of."

Darby arrived with everyone's drinks and passed them out. Stella lifted her pomegranate margarita into the air, and her teammates held their drinks up too.

"To team Beyond Amazing. Let's win this time," Stella said. "I know we are all tired of coming in second."

They tapped their drinks together. When Holly tapped her glass to Wagner's, their eyes met. His brown eyes pierced her light blue ones, and their intensity held her captive. But that was broken by Trivia Guy, reading the first question.

"What Italian fashion company's logo has interlocked *G's*?"

"So easy," Holly said. "Give it a seven, Joe."

"Okay, but what's the answer?" he asked.

"Gucci," Kali, Stella, and Holly said together, but quietly enough that the tables around them hopefully didn't hear.

Joe wrote down the answer and took it to the trivia guy. Wagner was keeping track of the score sheet, but he kept looking at Holly, eager to keep up their banter and to keep the conversation going. The shared jokes through his texts to Holly, and the comedy he had used tonight was the most fun, and relaxed interactions they'd had since they'd started working together. Maybe he'd pick up a hint soon, something tangible that would give him the courage to ask her out again.

"Holly," Wagner said. "do you remember the episode of *The Office* where Dwight says, "Today smoking is going to save lives, then tosses a lit cigarette into the trash can, catching it on fire?" he asked.

"Oh yeah. Then Michael runs out of his office screaming, 'It's happening.' Dwight yells, 'What's the procedure?' and total chaos breaks loose," Holly said. "I like how Angela goes to a filing cabinet behind her desk and opens a drawer to get her cat out of it. Oscar pulls the ceiling tiles out above his desk, then climbs up into the ceiling, and Angela starts screaming, '"Save me too. Take me with you.'"

Both Holly and Wagner laughed. "Yeah," Wagner said, "then Oscar says, 'You weigh too much. I can't pull you up,' then Angela throws her cat through the hole in the ceiling, thinking Oscar would catch it, but the cat comes flying back down and lands on Angela's desk."

Holly slapped the table. "Oh my gosh," Holly said. "And remember the episode when Jim dresses up like Dwight and imitates him all day?"

"Yoo-hoo!" Stella called from across the table. "I don't think you guys heard the question," she said in a singsong voice with a hint of sarcasm. "What year did World War Two start? We all agree it's 1939. If you and Wagner agree, we are turning it in."

Wagner and Holly nodded, trying to stifle their laughter. "That's right," Holly said. "Turn it in."

By round four, the teammates were almost finished with their second round of drinks, which had always been their limit and usually took them to the last round of questions. So far, their team had been holding steady in first place, and as long as they finished strong, they might finally pull away with a first-place win. The trivia guy began announcing the categories for the final round, then gave an update on team placement. When he called out team Beyond Amazing in first place, Holly and her team hooted, and hollered.

"Your final round categories are movies, records, chemistry, and classic literature. First question. "What prop from the *Wizard of Oz* movie was stolen?"

Holly leaned in toward her teammates and said, "The ruby slippers."

"Too obvious," Joe said.

"I don't know," Wagner said.

Stella shrugged. "What do you think, Kali?"

"I've never seen that movie," Kali admitted.

"You're kidding," Holly said. "It's one of my favorites. Okay, what do y'all want to put?"

"What about the oil can?" Joe suggested.

"Holly, what do you think?" Wagner asked.

"Honestly, I don't know. I was just guessing. Anyone else got any ideas?"

The teammates shook their heads.

"You want to go with the oil can?" Stella asked. "Since Joe thinks the ruby slippers would be too obvious of an answer for round four."

"Sure," Kali said.

"Whatever you guys want," Wagner said.

"Give it a one," Stella said.

Joe got up, walked up to the trivia guy, and gave him the answer sheet. A few minutes later, Trivia Guy gave the answer. "The question was, What prop from the movie *The Wizard of Oz* was stolen? And——it was," he said drawing out the words, "the ruby slippers."

Holly put her head on the table while the others let loose with some choice language. Then the teammates all looked at Joe.

"The oil can," Stella said. "If Bane of Your Existence got that answer right and gave it a seven, and they beat us tonight, Joe . . ." She let her voice trail off.

"You're in trivia time-out for the rest of the night," Kali said.

"Trivia time-out?" Joe asked.

"Ha, ha," Stella said. "No one's been in trivia time-out since Holly gave that goofy answer months ago when she convinced us the Caesar salad was invented in Rome. But it was first created in Tijuana, Mexico, by some guy named Caesar Cardini, remember? That was the first time we put anyone in trivia time-out. Because Holly said to give it a seven."

"But we only used our one on this last question," Joe argued.

"Doesn't matter," Stella said. "This is round four; the stakes are higher. And, besides, who wants to steal an oil can, for God's sake?"

Stella rolled her eyes. Holly and Kali snickered. Joe lifted both hands in surrender.

Wagner placed a hand over his heart, then sang, "If I only had a heart," which caused everyone but Joe to burst into laughter.

When it got down to the end of round four, the trivia guy announced the last question before the final bonus. "What are the three colors that make up visible light?"

The teammates began to argue over the answer.

"But red and yellow make orange, and blue and yellow make green," Holly explained as the argument continued. "So that would mean the three colors would be red, yellow, and blue, because blue and red make purple."

"No," Wagner said. "It's not talking about making colors. It's light, as in the electromagnetic spectrum. I promise you guys the answer is red, green, and blue. Trust me on this."

"What point value do we have left?" Joe asked.

"You're still in trivia time-out," Stella interjected. "We have a seven left, and if we miss this question, I know we won't be in first place going into the final bonus."

Everyone looked at Wagner. "I know it's right," he said confidently.

"Do you want to wager money on it?" Kali asked.

Wagner shrugged. "Sure. How much?"

Kali laughed. "I was kidding. Just wanted to see how confident you really were with this answer."

Kali wrote down red, green, and blue, circled the seven for the point value, and turned their answer in. Team Beyond Amazing then sat, fingers crossed, until, finally, Trivia Guy revealed the answer. When he did, Wagner jumped from his seat, followed by the rest of his teammates as they high-fived each other across the table. Then he turned to Holly, who was beaming at him, and he smiled down at her. She lifted her fist for a fist bump. It was casual and chummy, friend-like, but she kinda wished he would pick her up and spin her around. Maybe if they came in first, that might be appropriate.

It would be a major deal to beat Bane of Your Existence after playing trivia every Tuesday night for more than a year and coming in second or third, or at least one time fourth place. Winning tonight would mean something to them and be the perfect reason for a celebration. Maybe Wagner would even take a chance and ask Holly out. Last year when he'd asked her out, she'd told him she had other plans. And she hadn't lied to him; she really did have plans, but afterwards her actions made it clear that she just wasn't interested. But now things had most definitely changed. Well, she'd see how it went. After all, they still needed to ace the bonus round to make sure they held strong in first place.

Trivia Guy's voice boomed from his microphone. "Final bonus," he said. "Name the five most abundant elements in the universe, specifically in the Milky-Way."

Kali's eyes grew wide. Stella looked back and forth at her teammates.

Holly said, "Oxygen?"

Wagner nodded. "That's one. Also, hydrogen, helium, carbon, and I think neon."

"Neon?" Kali questioned.

"I think he's right," Joe said.

"What part of trivia time-out don't you get, Joe?" Stella asked.

"Quit picking on Joe," Holly said. "I'm beginning to think you have a crush on him."

Holly laughed. Stella gave her a don't-be-daft look.

Quickly, Kali ran up to Trivia Guy and handed in their answer sheet.

As Darby came around to pass out their checks, Trivia Guy was about to reveal the answer to the bonus round. When he read off the list of elements, and they realized they'd gotten five answers correct, they all jumped from their seats. Trivia Guy announced the top four teams, and after he proclaimed team Beyond Amazing in first, the teammates cheered. Stella squealed, "We did it! We just beat Bane of Your Existence!"

Holly made her way around the table and hugged Stella, then Kali jumped in. The guys were high-fiving each other, then Stella and Kali joined. Still fueled by the excitement of finally winning the first-place fifty-dollar gift card, Holly came back around to her side of the table, and hugged Wagner. At first it was just from the pure adrenaline, she felt rushing through her veins, but he held her just a bit longer than was common for a celebration hug. When she pulled away, he held her gaze, and his lips parted in a sweet smile.

"You knew the answer," Holly said. "You are so incredibly smart, Wagner."

He let out a little chuckle. "Uh, thanks," he said. "Um, I was, um, just thinking maybe we could get together sometime and watch *The Office?*"

Holly nodded. "Yeah, that would be fun."

It was vague. Not really a date. There had been no day or time suggested, only a maybe and the idea of a get-together sometime that could mean everything or nothing. But Holly knew it was definitely the beginning of something.

24

To Prank or Not to Prank

Holly felt anxious going in to work on Thursday, which was April Fools' Day. She and Wagner had been joking around about it for the past three days, and she wasn't sure what the day held. For most of the week he'd been texting in the morning to see if he could make her coffee, but there had been no text that day. She was feeling a little on guard and had made the decision to arrive earlier than usual. That way, she could maybe feel more prepared for whatever April Fools' prank might await her.

She'd brought with her a brand-new packet of rainbow-colored sticky notes so she could put them all over Stella's computer and workspace, hopefully before Stella got there. But she couldn't help but wonder what schemes Wagner might be up to.

After walking through the office doors, she moved quickly through the open areas to the spot where her and Stella's desks sat. She pulled the pad of sticky notes out of her purse and began placing the rainbow-colored papers all over Stella's chair and on every inch of flat space on her desk. She looked at her work, then quickly took a photo; it would be something funny to post about on the *Beyond* Blog and call it 'Office Shenanigans on April Fools.' She could even use it as one of their social-media posts. After taking the photo, she sat at her desk and opened her laptop to check her email.

Before Holly could read the first email, Marla walked through the doors and went into the conference room. A moment later Joe did the same. Holly turned back to her email and finished reading and replying to most. Then Kali walked in and went to her desk, which was on the opposite side of the office, near Wagner's. Holly got up and walked over to speak to Kali. On her way past the conference room, she could hear Marla and Joe talking about ordering supplies from Amazon.

"Hey," Holly said as she approached Kali.

"Hey. What's up?"

Holly raised her eyebrows. "Um," she said, tilting her head to the side, "just seeing if anything's different today." She gave Kali an expectant look.

"Different?"

Holly nodded. "Yeah, since it's April Fools' Day."

Kali started laughing. "I think you're making too much of a big deal about today. It's just a normal day. No one's going to jump out at you in a clown suit. That only happens on *The Ellen Show*."

"Yeah, probably," Holly said.

Kali started looking through the notes on her desk, so Holly told her she'd talk to her later. She was turning around to walk back to her desk when she saw Stella walk in. Holly stopped to watch Stella's reaction when she saw what was waiting for her. As soon as Stella saw the rainbow-covered surface of her workstation, she started screaming.

"Joe!" Stella yelled. "Joe, I know this was you! I know you're somewhere watching. Get over here now and take *all* of this off of my desk."

Joe and Marla walked out of the conference room looking both confused and annoyed.

When Marla saw what Stella had been yelling about, she cracked a smile, shook her head, then turned to go into her office. Before she did, she told Joe to make sure to get the Amazon order placed after he handled Stella's desk situation. Joe walked over to take a closer look at Stella's desk.

Stella stood, hands on hips, and head cocked to one side, waiting to hear what Joe had to say. "I know you wanted to get back at me for teasing you about being in trivia time-out, but this might be a little too much." She pointed to her desk. "Please get it off so I can get to work."

Joe started laughing. "Is there a pot of gold under that rainbow? Maybe the ruby slippers?" he asked.

"It's not that funny, Joe," Stella said.

Holly walked over and stood next to Joe.

"April Fools'," Holly said.

Joe's mouth flew open. Stella looked from Joe to Holly, and a look of shock came across her face.

"Holly?" Stella asked.

Holly nodded. "Let Joe off the hook. It was my prank. I got here early. I'll help you take it all down."

Joe pointed to Stella. "A lesson to you," he said with a smile. "Be careful who you sit next to. Can you really trust her, *or* should you really trust me?" He grinned. "No hard feelings, huh, Stella." He clapped Holly on the back. "Good one, Holly."

He gave Holly a thumbs-up. "Excellent. Priceless. This made my morning," he said, snickering, before he walked away.

Holly started removing the Post-it notes, trying to stack them carefully so she could reuse them. Stella started helping her, and within a few minutes they had the stack of rainbow-colored Post-its somewhat back in order.

"I have to admit," Stella said, "it was a funny joke, and something I'd never expect from my sweet Holly."

She leaned in and gave Holly a shoulder nudge. Then Marla opened her office door and made an announcement. "Is everyone here?" she asked. "I have a surprise for you guys."

Just then Wagner walked into the office. He glanced at Holly, waved, and continued toward his desk.

Marla walked out of her office. "And," she continued, "I'm going to tell you all what the surprise is over lunch today. We have a reservation at noon at Le Colonial in Buckhead Village. Some of you can ride with me; we'll take two cars."

A few hoots from the guys rang out. Some applause.

"Get back to work on copy editing your sections, but let's plan to meet at the office entrance at eleven forty-five. Then we'll head over," Marla said before walking back into her office and closing the door.

"Oh my gosh," Stella said. "I wrote about that restaurant for one of our blogs right after it opened. I've always wanted to go there. It's, like, really nice and really expensive."

"Oooh," Holly said. "Maybe not too expensive for lunch, I hope."

Stella lifted her shoulders. "I guess Marla's going to use the business credit card. It sounds like she's treating everyone to a special lunch."

Holly moved to sit at her own desk, then turned to Stella. "Could it be an April Fools' joke?" she asked.

Stella cracked up. "Nah, I don't think Marla would joke about something like that, but now you have me wondering."

Holly turned on her laptop, then reached for a pen and her notepad to jot down things to remember to add to her blog. Her container of pens was gone. She looked more carefully at the surface of her desk. All of her notepads, along with her stapler, tape, scissors, and everything else were gone. Also, her desk looked clean; all the smudges and coffee stains had disappeared. Had the cleaning staff gone a little extra and removed all of her stuff? Suddenly she realized what was really going on.

She turned to look at Stella and gave her a sarcastic stare. "Stella! Don't act all innocent," she said.

"What?"

"You know what! Give me back all of my stuff."

Stella moved her chair closer to Holly's desk and looked at it. "I swear, Holly. I didn't take your stuff."

Holly decided to look inside the side drawers. She pulled both of them out, but her pens and notepads weren't there, just her extra makeup bag and hairbrush. Next, she opened the center drawer, which was filled with M&M's.

"Stella," she cried. "Look."

Stella rolled her chair over to Holly to see what she wanted to show her. Then she started to laugh. "That's hilarious," Stella said.

"But where is my stuff?"

Holly pulled the drawer out further and saw a note. She took it out and read it out loud.

"It says, 'Because you're so M&Mazing.'" Holly looked inside the drawer again. "But wait, there's another note."

Stella had grabbed her cell phone and was snapping photos of the drawer of M&M's.

Holly read the second note. This one says, 'I appreciate you a choco-lot.' And there's another note way in the back of the drawer." She pulled the drawer open as far as it would go, reached into the back to retrieve the third note, and read it to Stella. "'Thanks for being M&M-mesmerizing. Look under your desk.'"

"Oh, my God, Holly. We know who did this, right?" Stella asked. "We are both on the same page here, aren't we?"

"I think so," Holly said. She got out of her chair, then crawled under her desk to see what was there. Stella couldn't help taking a photo of Holly on her hands and knees under her desk.

"What do you see?" Stella asked.

"All of my pencils, pens, notes, stapler, tape, and scissors. It's all inside two bags that are taped to the underside of the desk."

Holly pulled down the two large Ziploc bags filled with her things, crawled out from under the desk, and set the bags on top of her desk, where she started to unpack everything and put them back in order. Then she saw another note folded up inside one of the bags and took it out.

"There's another note," she told Stella.

"This is so good," Stella said. "Seriously, Wagner has my vote for sure. Don't you *dare* think about giving Garrison another chance, no matter how much he apologizes. What does it say?"

Holly looked at Stella. "First of all, you know I'm not considering anything that has to do with Garrison, and second, do we really know this was Wagner's doing?"

"Uh, yeah, I think we do. Read the note, girl."

"April Fools'. I hope you don't mind too much," the note began. "I couldn't resist playing a prank after how much we laughed this week over some funny April Fools' Day jokes. And I cleaned your desk and your drawer before putting the M&M's in there, by the way. I didn't want you to pop one into your mouth and be, like, Gross, what the heck is this," and pull out fuzz or some unknown goo when taking a bite. I know things have been hectic lately, but once the summer issue releases on the twenty-seventh, I wanted to ask if you'd make it a date. Will you come over and watch *The Office* with me over dinner? We can celebrate the magazine's summer release, and your cover story, of course, and enjoy a nice evening together. And, by the way, the reason for the M&M's is—well, Holly, you color my world." She read it out loud to Stella. "And it's signed, 'Wagner.'"

Stella's mouth was agape as she sat frozen and unblinking. When she finally moved, she said, "I don't know what to say. It's got to be the most romantic thing I've ever heard and seen. These M&Ms in your drawer have got to be, like, magic romantic beans. Give me some." Stella reached into the drawer, grabbed a handful, and shoveled them into her mouth. "Seriously," she said once she finished chewing. "We could, like, bag these up and sell them to women who are looking for their Prince Charming. Magic romance beans, like in *Jack and the Beanstalk.*"

Holly cracked up. Both girls started laughing hysterically. Holly snorted.

"You are going to say yes, aren't you?" Stella asked. "Tell him that you'll go to his place for dinner that night, right?"

"I will," Holly answered. "I just feel like it should be done in an interesting way. I mean, look how much trouble he went to. It's a prank, but like a proposal too. Remember getting those cute proposals back in high school?"

Stella shrugged. "Eh, the boys' moms or sisters used to help them with those. This is all Wagner."

25

The future's So Bright I Gotta Wear Shades

Stella helped Holly dump the candy into the two Ziploc bags that had held Holly's stuff. Then they sat and looked at the mountain of M&Ms.

"That was sweeter than any floral arrangement could ever be," Stella said. "I mean, just think about the careful planning that it took to pull that off. It's very impressive."

"I really love flowers, but I agree. This was extra," Holly said.

Holly snapped a few photos of the giant bags of M&M's sitting on her desk, then texted one of the pics to Wagner.

Best prank ever!

Glad you liked it.

I did. You might need to keep watch; something might be about to jump out and get you too.

I'm going to take my chances. Maybe I do want something to jump out and get me.

He'd added a laughing emoji. But when Holly read that last text, she almost choked on her own spit. He was really flirting; *they* were really flirting. This was really happening. She did have a thing for Wagner after all, no more denying it. Holly set her phone down and bit her lip. She leaned back in her chair and got Stella's attention.

"For real," Holly said. "I don't want to just walk up to him and say, 'Hey, thanks for the dinner invite. Yeah, I'll be there.' I want to answer with something fun."

"We could get an office pet, like a dog, then you could write a note and stick it under its collar and tell it to 'Go find Wagner.' I saw that in a movie once. The movie was based on a Nicholas Sparks book, and you know how romantic those are."

"What? I'm not going to buy a dog for the office, just so I can pass cute notes to Wagner."

"Maybe borrow a dog for the day."

"I need to think of something that's kinda like one of those prom-proposal type deals. What time is it in England right now?"

Stella shook her head. "Don't know."

"I'm thinking out loud. I can look it up. Ten a.m. here is . . . Okay, so they are five hours ahead of us. My cousin Denim had some type of cute proposal thing happen to her that she loved before her junior prom. She could be back at her flat after rehearsals or auditions or whatever she's been doing lately. I'm going to text her."

Hey, Denim. Hope your day has gone well. I'm at work and I will have to tell you about the funniest, yet sweetest prank that was pulled on me today for AFD. I want to reply to it in a fun way, but need your help. Remember that prom proposal that you thought was so fun? Tell me about how it worked again.

She got an answer right away.

Hey, cuz. Great day here. Sounds like a good one for you too. We start rehearsals officially tomorrow. I got the part I wanted, and I'm psyched. I think you are thinking about when my then boyfriend took me to lunch and had the waiter put a note along with the prom tix on a holder thing that was stuck into my burger. When it arrived at the table it was such a cute way for him to ask me to prom.

That was it! I'll call you this weekend. Congratulations on the part. Have a great night. Love you, girl.

Holly turned back to Stella. "I've got it. And if I can make this work, it will happen during lunch today."

Stella gave her a thumbs-up. "You go, girl."

* * * * * *

Later, when the office crew left for the restaurant, Kali and Stella rode with Holly in her car, and the guys got a ride with Marla. After parking, the six of them walked together down the sidewalk. Now that Wagner was most definitely on her radar, Holly was almost drooling at the way he looked in his Wayfarer-style black sunglasses. With the increased attention she was paying Wagner, she thought he looked stylish, dashing even. And she was finding him to be much more than a smart geek; she was entranced.

When they all got onto the elevator that would take them up to Le Colonial, everyone removed their sunglasses, and Holly glanced at Wagner. He turned to look at her too. He smiled. She smiled back at him and felt a warmth course through her that lit up all of her senses.

After walking into Le Colonial, they each oohed and aahed over the tropical Asian decor. It was like a French-Vietnamese palace. Large palm trees and elegant orchids filled the space along with props and furnishings that gave everything a 1920s feel. The attention to Asian details throughout was impressive. The hostess led the group to a large round table. Marla sat down first, and Wagner ended up between Marla and Holly. The lighting was dim. The candle on their table flickered against the dark wood of the walls, creating even more of a sense that they'd stepped back in time.

Marla got everyone's attention and spoke. "So, this lunch today is my treat," she began. "It's been three years since I started Beyond, and I've just now begun to feel like I can breathe a little. The latest issue already feels like a success. Michael and I came here a few months ago for a dinner date, and I loved the food and the style of this place. Even though it has a Vietnamese-theme, the chef is French. Of course, you guys know that Vietnam used to be a French colony, which is why there's a French flair to the food. The food here is magnificent; it definitely feels like a Michelin-star restaurant, the kind that you might find in Europe. I thought we'd first order from the small plates so that everyone could sample something from them, but feel free to order whatever you want for lunch. And I'm even having a cocktail, so if you want to indulge a little, go ahead."

A waiter arrived and handed each of them a menu, leaving a few cocktail menus on the table too. Holly made a note to remember the waiter so she could sneak away at some point and give him the note and tell him her plan. After they placed their lunch orders, she'd excuse herself to the "restroom" in hopes of tracking him down to explain what she wanted them to do.

A few minutes later, a beautiful Asian girl came by to take their orders for the appetizers. She described some of the dishes on the small-plate menu, and to Holly it all sounded incredible.

"The Goi Cuon," the girl explained, "is a jumbo shrimp roll, rice noodles, bean sprouts, lettuce, and aromatic herbs, with a creamy peanut sauce for dipping. Banh Cuon is Hanoi steamed rice and a crepe with farm chicken, wood-ear mushrooms, and bean sprouts. That one is served with a Nuoc Cham sauce.

Kali asked about the vegetable rolls, and the waitress replied, "The Cha Gio Chay is a crispy vegetable roll with taro root, bean threads, aromatic herbs, and lettuce and it comes with a tamarind sauce for dipping."

Marla ordered several small plates so they could each get a sample since everything sounded scrumptious. For her lunch entrée, Holly had decided on the Banh Mi Thit Nuong, which was a heritage pork shoulder covered in a spicy curry aioli with pickled carrot and daikon cucumber inside a crispy baguette with a house salad on the side. When the appetizers arrived, everyone snapped open their wooden chopsticks, and plates began being passed around. When Holly and Wagner each had a shrimp roll between their chopsticks, aimed for a dip in the peanut sauce, their hands bumped, and Holly's shrimp roll fell into the sauce. The slight touch from Wagner's hand sent a warm glow through her middle that crept up to her throat, and she blushed.

Holly giggled when her shrimp roll fell. "Sorry," she said to Wagner. He snapped his chopsticks at her in a playful manner.

A different waiter, this time an older male, arrived to take their entrée orders. Marla ordered a spicy Vietnamese Margarita that she said was made from peach puree, Thai simple syrup, and fresh lime. "It sounds yummy," Marla said.

Stella ordered the same drink, and Holly decided on the Saigon 75, which was made with gin, fresh lemon, simple syrup, and Paul Chevalier champagne. Kali and the guys ordered beers. Soon everyone's drinks arrived. Holly's came in a champagne-style glass with a curled lemon peel fixed to the side. Marla's and Stella's drinks were topped with a cube of fresh pineapple and a cherry, and each glass of beer was accompanied by a slice of fresh orange.

Marla called for a toast, and everyone lifted their glasses. "I want to toast each one of you," she said as she locked eyes with each staffer around the table. "Most of you have been with me from the beginning, and I am so grateful that you've stuck with it. You've believed in my goals right alongside me, trusted me, and helped me keep going on a daily basis. And now . . . " She paused. "Now I know we've made it big!"

Everyone clinked their glasses together, sipped, then sat their drinks down. Marla continued. "There are several things I want to share with you that I'm excited about, and I hope you all will be too. First, I've been asked to be a guest on *'In a New York Minute.'*"

There were several gasps, with Stella seeming to be particularly thrilled. Holly knew this news was coming, as she'd heard it straight from Bradley herself. But she'd kept it a secret since she wasn't sure it was something she was supposed to pass along to Marla or mention to the others. And she was glad she had kept quiet, since it was probably better that Bradley had asked Marla herself.

"Michael and I will leave for New York the day before the summer issue releases," continued Marla. "So on the morning of the twenty-seventh, I will be at Bradley's studio waiting to go on air with her, and the summer issue of *Beyond* will be in most newsstands across Manhattan. As well as throughout Atlanta and other major Southern cities."

Kali lifted her glass, and everyone toasted to this exciting news.

"And there's more good news," Marla went on. "Since word has gotten out that Bradley will be the subject of our cover story, we've gotten more calls from businesses wanting to purchase advertising. Lots of full-page-ad requests are coming in. And once the magazine is released, there will be even more, I'm sure. So I've decided that since we need to hire more employees, I'll be going to SCAD in Savannah to interview students who will be graduating next month."

Holly nodded as she listened and thought that Marla would definitely find some talented students at the School of Art and Design.

Marla looked around the table. She tossed a strand of her long dark hair over one shoulder. "You guys have been my rocks," she continued. "I'm going to do my best to find the perfect fit with these new hires. And I want you guys to welcome them, help show them the ropes, and make them feel at home."

"Of course," Holly said. The others all agreed.

Marla continued. "I'll be gone most of next week since the interviews are set up over multiple days," she said with a smile. "I know most of you think I work too much, and this will be a work trip, as will be my time in New York the week after that. But Michael is going with me on both trips, and next week, he wants us to stay in Savannah an extra day for sightseeing. Then he wants us to go to Tybee Island for the rest of the weekend." She leaned back in her seat and pursed her lips as tears welled in her eyes. Emotion seemed to overwhelm her as she struggled not to cry. After she pulled herself together, she said, "I know I can leave the office in good hands."

Everyone at the table nodded. Kali reached over and rubbed Marla's shoulder. "We won't let you down, Marla," she said.

"We will work extra hard to make sure everything will run just as smoothly as if you were there," Stella added.

"I'll need you guys to answer the phone in my office, please," said Marla. "And I thought over lunch today, we could toss around ideas for future stories since I won't be conducting conference-room meetings while I'm gone next week. So if anyone wants to throw out ideas for this fall's cover story, go ahead. Or if you have ideas for other articles, let's think on those during lunch. After all," she said with a laugh, "this is a work-expense lunch; we might as well get some work done."

Everyone chuckled. Then Holly stood and excused herself to go to the "restroom." Stella did the same. It was now or never, Holly thought, as she looked around for someone on the waitstaff. Hopefully she could get someone to find the young girl who had described some of the appetizers to them. Stella scooted up behind Holly and got her attention.

"What's the plan?" Stella asked.

"I want to find one of our waiters. I have a note in my purse, and I want them to put it on some type of stick; or garnish or find some way to display it in some way on Wagner's plate. But I really want the young girl to be the one to deliver his food to him."

"Why?" Stella asked.

They moved into the hallway that led to the restrooms. Then Holly answered. "Because she's young and pretty, and it might be fun to make it look like she's flirting with him and maybe giving him her number."

"But isn't everyone going to want to know what the note says?" Stella asked.

"There she is," Holly said. She walked quickly toward the waitress, who was walking toward the front of the restaurant. She watched as the girl went to the patio area to speak with a group of diners at a table. Holly waited near the entrance.

When the girl left the table, she walked toward Holly and stopped. "Do you need something, ma'am?" she asked.

Holly nodded. "I have a special request. I have a note for someone at our table. It's kind of like a joke. You know, an April Fools' joke. But instead of a joke, it's really more of an answer to a question. And I want him to receive my answer in a special and unique way." Holly tilted her head to one side, bit her lip, and, with a pleading look, she asked, "Do you think you could be the one to bring him his meal?"

The young girl was smiling at Holly and nodded.

"Okay," Holly said. "So, I was wondering if you or someone in the kitchen could add this note to his order." She dug the note from her purse, folded it in half, and handed it to the girl. "Maybe put this on a clip or attach it to a stick like a garnish for his food?"

The girl looked at the note Holly had given her but didn't unfold it. She nodded and asked, "Which one should this go to?"

"It's for the guy who is sitting next to me on my left. His name is Wagner, and he ordered, I think, the spicy-chicken stir-fry."

The girl nodded, slipped the note into her pocket, and walked away. Quickly, Holly went back to the women's restroom and found Stella inside. "Okay," Holly said. "Operation April Fools' is a go."

"But what does the note say? And do you think Wagner will read it out loud?"

Holly shook her head. "I don't think he will. I wrote, 'I'm looking forward to spending more time alone with you. XO, Holly.'"

Stella's eyes grew wide. "Well, okay, girlfriend," she said. "Let's get back to it. I can't wait to see what happens next."

26

That's a Lovely Orchid

The girls hurried back to their table. The conversation had turned to discussions about who should be on the fall cover.

Kali said, "Michelle Obama."

Marla nodded. "Excellent choice. I can try."

"Stacey Abrams," Stella offered.

Marla shook her head. "No, not after our last two covers. We've now had women on our magazine covers who've been much more in the public eye outside of Georgia, but she's perfect for an inside article."

"What about Doctor Kizzmekia Corbett?" Holly offered. "The female doctor who was one of the leading scientists who developed the Moderna version of the COVID-19 vaccine back in 2020?"

Marla nodded. "I like it."

Their food had arrived, and plates were set in front of each of them except for Wagner and Joe. Marla realized that they were still waiting and put her fork down. Holly had been waiting too. After Marla set her fork down, the young waitress that Holly had given the note to walked up to their table with a plate that held a white orchid. Sticking through the petals was a tropical-looking wooden stick with the folded note attached beneath the flower. The waitress walked up behind Joe and went to set the plate down in front of him. Holly fell into a panic as she envisioned Joe reading the note about her wanting some alone time with him. Stella saw the look on Holly's face and quickly asked, "Is that what you ordered, Joe?"

The waitress glanced at Holly and caught her eye. Holly shook her head slightly. Joe was in mid-sentence with his answer as another waiter arrived with his food and quickly placed it in front of him. The young girl moved behind Wagner, reached around, and set the correct plate in front of him.

"Wow," Kali said. "You got an orchid."

"It looks like you got a note too," Joe added. "What does it say? Maybe I *should* have ordered that."

Wagner removed the stick and tugged the note from the bottom half, leaving the flower intact. He set the stick with the flower aside and opened the folded letter. A sly smile tugged at the corners of his mouth. He cleared his throat and maybe even blushed a little. It was dim inside the restaurant, so Holly wasn't sure. Then he tucked the note into the front pocket of his button-down shirt and took a bite of his food.

"Wagner," Joe said. "Seriously, man, what is the note for? Or who is it from? Are you going to tell us?"

Everyone stopped eating and looked at Wagner.

Wagner shook his head. "It's personal," he said.

Kali giggled. "That waitress is really attractive. Maybe she gave Wagner her number?"

Marla looked at Wagner, who was smiling while picking up his glass. He seemed to be enjoying this but was determined not to share his note with his office mates. Holly moved her hand up onto the table close to Wagner's plate and rested it there. When Wagner picked up his knife, his hand brushed hers. He smiled but didn't turn to look at her. Instead, he made a point of brushing his hand against hers again; this next time it was on purpose.

Marla might have noticed what was going on between Holly and Wagner, but if she did, she kept it to herself and drew the conversation back to the fall issue, and soon everyone was back to talking about work topics.

* * * * * *

On their way back to the office after lunch, there might have been a few stolen glances between Wagner and Holly, but the others were none the wiser. Once they were back at the office and had gotten back to work, a text from Wagner popped up on Holly's phone.

Best AFD note ever! Great surprise. And ten out of ten for presentation.

I am glad you liked it.

More than liked it.

Holly let out a sigh; his text had stirred a flutter in her stomach. She might have swooned a little, but she was not going to reply. He was getting to her, and she wanted to keep things professional at work. She set her phone aside and finished her blog post.

When it was time to leave for the day, she walked out the door with Stella by her side. Stella followed Holly over to her car. She waited as Holly unlocked her door and opened it before she asked about the note. "Spill," Stella said. "What did Wagner say about the note? Did he say anything to you?"

"He did." Holly's grin was wide; it lit up her whole face.

Stella raised an eyebrow. "And . . ." she said, impatiently.

"He sent me a text letting me know it was the best April Fools' Day surprise ever and that the presentation was a ten out of ten. I texted back that I was glad he liked it, and he texted that he *more* than liked it."

Stella drew in a breath. "Shiiii. . . ."

Instead of completing the word, she gave Holly a wide-eyed look.

"I don't know what to say," Stella finally said.

"There's nothing to say," Holly answered. "We should keep things professional at work. Besides, the date is several weeks away still."

"I know, but holy smoke show," Stella said. "The question is, How hot will it be when you two finally get together? What if he's too much of a gentleman for you, and you end up ripping his clothes off?"

They laughed, then Holly got into her car and told Stella she'd talk to her later.

When Holly got home and walked inside her apartment, all the curtains had been shut, and it was completely dark. Then she heard sobbing coming from Lofton's room. Lofton's door was cracked open, and Holly knocked gently.

"Lofton," she called. "Is everything okay?"

"No," was all Lofton said.

"Can I come in?" Holly asked.

"I guess."

It was all she got in response, so Holly pushed the door open to find Lofton in the dark, in bed, and crying. Holly dropped her bag and rushed to the side of Lofton's bed. Padre had been curled up next to Lofton. He arched his back, started purring, and began making invisible biscuits on the duvet.

"Are you sick? Do you need to go to the hospital?" Holly asked. Her voice was filled with panic.

"I'm not sick. It's. . . It's. . ."

More sobbing.

"What can I do? Please, Lofton, let me help," Holly begged, then sat next to Lofton and put an arm around her shoulder. Lofton sat up, leaned into Holly, and sobbed.

"I want to help," Holly said. "What can I do?"

Lofton sniffed loudly. "It's Neilson," she said. "A captain for Delta. I'd been seeing him." She wiped her nose with the back of her hand. "He was the reason I'd gotten a better schedule with the European flights. He filled in a little over a month ago for a pilot on my flight to Washington DC. I'd been working business class on that flight, and I guess he noticed me."

Lofton sat up more and leaned back on her pillow. Holly leaned against the headboard and waited for Lofton to continue. Padre made his way over to Holly and sat on her leg.

"When we arrived in DC, we had a four-hour layover before the flight went on to Boston," Lofton explained. "He started talking to me during the flight a little and then after we deplaned, he asked if I wanted to get something to eat with him. He said he knew a great place near Lafayette Square. I was less familiar with DC, so I just said, 'Sure.'" Anyway, we had a great time during the layover, and I thought he was single, because he wasn't wearing a wedding ring."

"Oh, Lofton," Holly said. Her hand flew up to cover her mouth.

"Once we got back home to Atlanta, he asked if he could see me again, and I said yes. It was really just a low-key lunch date. We met at Krog Street Market, walked a little on the Beltline, talked a lot, grabbed some lunch, and talked some more. It was all casual, and he was nice and said he enjoyed talking to me. That's when he told me he was getting divorced. That his wife wanted him home more in order to be with their two boys, who were nine and eleven. But he'd told her he needed a certain number of hours of flying time to stay on track for the salary he wanted, the best flight schedule, a good retirement, and so forth. Things had apparently gotten worse at home, and she asked him to leave and filed for divorce. So by the time I met him, he was living in a one-bedroom apartment in Vinings."

Lofton reached over and took a tissue from the box by her nightstand, wiped her eyes, then blew her nose. "I'm so sorry, Lofton," Holly said.

"I'm a dumbass," Lofton said. "I thought his divorce was about to be final and that he was falling in love with me, especially after he got me a better flight schedule so I could be with him on the red-eye flights to Europe. We had a great time exploring London and Paris together. Then on this last trip to Greece, he was acting funny. I knew something was wrong, but he wouldn't tell me what. Then after we got home today, he pulled me aside in the airport and told me that his wife wanted to work things out. He said he'd decided to go back to her and try again. The fact that he was able to just walk away from me like there was nothing between us . . ." She shook her head. "It ripped my heart in half. It felt like he had torn my heart out of my chest and stomped on it until it stopped beating."

Holly pulled Lofton in close and held her.

"I couldn't even drive home," Lofton said. "I got an Uber. My car's still at the airport. I don't know if I can ever leave this apartment again. I don't want to. And I can't go back to work. I know my old crew will know what happened. I know why I wasn't scheduled for an upcoming flight this week; he must have told his regular flight crew I wouldn't be back or something."

"This pilot is scum of the earth," Holly told her.

"He's actually a captain." Lofton corrected her.

"I don't care what his rank is. He used you. It's not your fault, Lofton. He was dishonest with you."

"I should have known better," Lofton said. "I should have been more cautious, especially with a captain who was more than ten years older than me and claiming he was getting a divorce. I don't know what came over me, but at the time it felt so romantic. It was like living in a dream that was too good to be true—and it most definitely was."

Holly put her palms on each of Lofton's cheeks and looked into her eyes. "I know you feel rotten. And it's going to feel like this for a while but use this as a lesson. Don't see this as an end but as a beginning for you. I guarantee you are smarter and wiser now. You've been burned, so you won't be putting your hand on a hot stove anymore. Listen, we've got the weekend. We can stay in and watch movies, order takeout, or go out and do something fun, whatever you want. I'm here for you. And when you start to feel a little better, we'll go get your car. And I think you should talk to your flight crew supervisor about getting back on your former schedule."

Lofton nodded. "Thanks, Holly."

"Of course," Holly said. She looked at the clock on Lofton's nightstand. "I know it's only seven, but why don't you get some sleep, and we'll talk more in the morning."

27
It's Almost That Time . . .

Two weeks later, Lofton was back to her usual carefree self, having decided she'd learned a valuable life lesson. She'd even gone back to work with her old Delta crew, working flights to Dallas, Orlando, Chicago, and a few boring cities here and there. She'd made a pact with Holly to talk more, especially about who she was interested in dating, so that together they'd figure things out. After all, what were roommates, former sorority sisters, and girlfriends for? Holly had Lofton's back, and Lofton knew Holly was a loyal friend she could trust and confide in.

And for Holly, the end of the week was fast approaching. It was a time that she hoped would be filled with a lot of exciting things. It was Thursday morning, and the day before the summer issue would hit Barnes & Noble stores, grocery-store shelves, and newsstands across the Southeast, and those in and around Manhattan.

Marla got everyone's attention and called them all into the conference room for a quick meeting. Once everyone had taken a seat around the table, Marla said, "Tomorrow's the big day for *Beyond*. Michael and I are flying to New York this afternoon, and I'll be leaving work early in order to catch our flight. And, as you know, I'll be interviewed on Bradley's talk show at eleven tomorrow morning."

Everyone nodded.

"We're going to be watching," Kali said.

Marla turned around, opened the drawer behind her, pulled out the remote for the conference-room TV, and set it on the table.

"It will be on ABC," she said. "And one last thing." She opened the folder she'd brought in with her and pulled out five white envelopes. "Make sure to answer the phone in my office, please, and try not to let it go to voicemail." She started handing out the envelopes. "These are your bonus checks," she said. "They're good ones this time; you guys will be very pleased."

Joe was the first to open his. "Hot damn," he exclaimed.

Everyone chuckled. Stella and Holly looked at each other, eyes wide. Holly opened her envelope and slowly pulled out the check. As she looked at the amount, she started thinking she might buy the Prada bag she'd had her eye on. Or maybe something new to wear tomorrow night for her date with Wagner. She was definitely thinking about going shopping after she got off work later.

Her shopping daydream ended when everyone started to get up to leave. Wagner and Joe shook hands with Marla, thanking her for their bonuses. Kali went over to thank Marla as well and wished her the best during her interview. Then Stella and Holly took their turns.

After they got back to their workstations, Stella asked Holly if she was getting nervous about her date tomorrow night.

Holly shook her head. "No. But I might go shopping after work to look for something to wear. Do you want to go with me?"

"Sure," Stella said. She held up the envelope from Marla. "I should go ahead and deposit this into my account."

She pulled up her banking app on her phone, signed the back of her check, and snapped a photo, and Holly decided to do the same. Stella set her phone down, put the check into her purse, then asked Holly if she knew what Wagner had planned for tomorrow night.

Holly smiled. "He gave me his address and said he was going to cook for me," she said. "And after dinner we plan to watch *The Office*. I'm really excited."

"Do you know what he's going to cook? Or even if he can cook?"

"Uh, I guess I'll find out. He told me he was going to make a lemon Parmesan pasta with garden salad and French bread. And he said that maybe after dinner, we could bake some slice-and-bake chocolate chip cookies or pop some popcorn before we settle in to watch the show."

Stella looked impressed. She shimmied her shoulders a little then said, "After we settle in, hubba—hubba. Wow. Okay, then. So, he's not only a smart dresser, who is tall and good-looking with a cool job, but he cooks and has his own apartment. He sounds perfect on paper. I hope his furniture isn't, like, leftover frat-house stuff. Does he own a second set of sheets? Or more importantly does he have any skeletons in his closet?"

Holly snorted. "Skeletons in the closet? In fact, I don't know much about Wagner. Except from just being around him at work and at trivia."

Stella pulled up the *Beyond* website on her laptop. "Have you stalked his Instagram or read through his bio on the website? I've never looked at anyone else's bio except mine and Marla's. I want to read what Wagner's says."

Holly rolled her chair over to Stella's desk as Stella clicked the "About" section on the website, scrolling down to the listing for Wagner Stein, Podcast Editor, Host, and Website Technician. His photo popped up on the screen along with a short bio.

"It says he has a BS from Belmont University in audio engineering," Stella said. "He's currently working on his master's degree in audio engineering at Georgia Tech."

Stella looked at Holly. "Didn't know that."

"I wonder how he has time for grad school," Holly said.

"Maybe at night or on the weekends," Stella said before she continued reading. "And he's originally from New York and graduated from the Lawrenceville School in New Jersey. I wonder what that is. Why would he go to a school in New Jersey if he's from New York.?"

"I'll look up what the Lawrenceville School is," Holly said. She scooted back over to her desk and pulled up the school's website on her laptop. "It's a coeducational college-prep boarding school. Whoa, and the tuition is mind-blowingly expensive."

Stella grinned at Holly. "There is a lot to uncover tomorrow night—in more ways than one, my friend." She waggled her eyebrows playfully. "Skeletons or not, your evening should be interesting."

"I suppose so," Holly agreed.

Just then a UPS driver walked through the office doors. "Delivery," he called.

Holly and Stella got up and went over to find him taking a large box off his hand truck.

"Thank you," Stella said.

The UPS driver gave her a nod and said, "See you next time."

"Can you pick up the box?" Holly asked Stella.

Stella bent down and tried to lift it. "Can you get the other side? Where are strong men when you need them?" Stella said in a loud voice.

Within a minute, both Joe and Wagner were taking the box from Stella and Holly and placing it on top of the conference-room table.

"I guess chivalry isn't dead," Stella said to the guys.

"I guess this is probably what we all think it is," Holly said.

Stella nodded at Holly, then turned to Wagner and Joe. "Yep," she said. "You guys go get Marla. She's going to need these before she leaves for the airport."

Joe walked out of the room, and when he came back, both Kali and Marla were with him. Marla took a look at the box and let out a breath; her shoulders lifted then fell as the air left her lungs. "This is the moment of truth," she said. She took a pair of scissors from a nearby drawer, sliced through the tape on the outside of the box, then opened the flaps. "Gorgeous," she said when she saw the contents. She took some copies of the summer issue and held them out for the others to see. "Go ahead and have as many as you'd like," she said. "I'm taking some to New York. In fact, Michael will probably be here in the next thirty minutes to pick me up."

Once everyone had the number of copies they wanted, Holly walked up and pulled out five copies for herself. She'd mail two to her parents, keep the other two for posterity, and mail the other to Lydia as she'd promised. She opened one of the magazines and turned to the cover story. There in bold print was the headline Holly had suggested, and below that was her name. "Beauty and Boldness: How Bradley Banner Captured an Audience and Found Her Calling" by Holly Curtis.

Wagner walked over and offered his congrats to her, then he said, "I'm looking forward to celebrating with you tomorrow night."

Holly looked into his dark brown eyes, which were glinting with interest, and said, "So am I. Seven thirty, right?"

Wagner nodded. "Or a little earlier is fine too. Either works."

Holly smiled up at him, her light blue eyes sparkling with flirtation.

Most had headed back to their desks. Marla took the rest of the magazines from the box and set them on a shelf with the other back issues. Wagner excused himself to Holly and offered to break down the empty box, for Marla, while Holly went back to her desk, placing her copies of *Beyond* into her large tote.

A few minutes later, Michael walked through the office doors. He was wearing a navy jacket with a white button-down, tan pants, and tan shoes. His wavy blonde hair bounced a little with each step. With a bright smile, he waved to Stella and Holly as he passed their workstations. Then, ten minutes later, he and Marla passed through the office with Marla's suitcase in tow. Before she walked out of the office doors, she said, "Please remember to answer my phone before it goes to voicemail. I'll see you all next week. Have a great weekend." She waved goodbye then turned to leave.

Stella and Holly called out, "Have fun in New York," before Marla disappeared.

* * * * *

Around five, Kali stopped by Stella and Holly's desks to discuss photo-shoot locations for next week's blogs and social-media postings. Kali made a list of locations that she planned to photograph tomorrow. And then the girls began a discussion about going shopping and having dinner together at

Ponce Market after work. Holly checked in with Lofton to see if she wanted to meet them at Ponce. Lofton told her she was staying in because she had an early flight scheduled in the morning. And she told Holly she'd gotten a postcard from Denim that was sitting out on the kitchen counter.

Kali walked back to her desk to gather her things while Holly and Stella wrapped up what they'd been working on. When Holly and Stella began to pack up, the phone started to ring in Marla's office. Holly looked at her cell phone to see what time it was.

"It's already five thirty," Holly said. "Way past working time. We don't have to answer it this late, do we?"

But as the phone continued to ring, they could hear Joe and Kali arguing about whose turn it was to answer. Apparently, Joe lost the argument. A few seconds later, he walked out of Marla's office and in a loud voice called for Holly. "Hey, Holly!" Joe yelled. "Someone named Garrison Simmons is on the line for you and says it's urgent." Joe's voice seemed even louder as it rang out through the open-spaced office.

Holly stood and started walking toward Marla's office with Stella right behind her. Before Holly stepped into Marla's office, Stella said, "You don't have to take his call, Holly. And no matter how much he pleads or apologizes, he's not worth your time."

Wagner happened by and eyed Stella as she spoke.

Holly glanced back at Stella, walked into Marla's office, and took the phone from Joe. Holly had a feeling if Garrison had something to say to her that was on a personal note, he'd just DM her Instagram like he'd done after he'd sent the tulips. Those messages had stopped, so maybe he'd taken a hint that she wasn't going to give him another chance.

Joe left Holly in Marla's office and went to his desk, where he gathered his things and headed for the door. Kali had moved to the couch at the front so she could walk out with Holly and Stella. Wagner shut his computer down and went to stand in the doorway of Marla's office, next to Stella. Out of everyone, he seemed the most curious about the call.

A horrified expression formed on Holly's face. Her lower lip trembled as she said, "Okay, I'll do that now. Can you hold a moment while I tell my co-workers?" Holly lowered the receiver from her ear and turned to look at Stella. "Garrison got a call from Michael," Holly said, her voice shaking. "By the time his and Marla's plane landed, Marla was in a lot of pain. It might be her stomach; they aren't sure. But Michael has decided to take Marla straight to the hospital. And Garrison called to tell me that Marla has requested that I come to New York right now in case she can't make it to the show in the morning. I need a plane ticket, like, now."

Wagner went back to his desk and turned on his computer. His hands flew across the keys as he rapidly typed in what he was looking for. Stella reached out and rubbed Holly's arm. "Tell him you'll be there," Stella said. Holly turned around and finished speaking to Garrison, then hung up, before she walked over to where Stella stood in the doorway.

"Garrison said he would get the details from his driver and text me about which hospital they take Marla to," Holly said. "I think they must be on their way to one now."

By this time, Kali had made her way over to see what was wrong.

"It's Marla," Holly told her. "One of Garrison's drivers picked up Michael and Marla at the airport, and Marla was in a lot of pain. They think it's something with her stomach, but they don't know yet. They are taking her to a hospital now, and Marla wants me to fly to New York to do the show if she can't make it. Should I go alone?" Holly's eyes moved between Stella and Kali.

Wagner shut his computer down then stood and walked over to Holly. "I'll go with you," he said. "I've just booked two tickets to LaGuardia. The flight leaves at nine forty-five. I'll go home and pack a bag, then pick you up." Quickly, he gathered his things, slung his leather messenger bag over his shoulder, then started walking toward the door.

Holly stood silent for a few beats before she said, "Thanks, Wagner."

Stella turned to Holly and said, "Let me ride home with you. Kali, will you follow us to Holly's? Kali and I can help you pack."

"Sure," Kali answered.

On his way through the office door, Wagner turned around and said, "Someone text me Holly's address."

"Will do," Kali said. "See you there in a few."

The girls gathered their things and headed for the door. Holly looked at her friends and said, "I'm sorry, guys. It doesn't look like we'll be going shopping tonight after all."

28

Time to Go

When the three girls arrived at Holly's apartment, they rushed in together, and with panic in their voices started giving each other directions. Lofton came out of her room, followed by Padre, who ran under the sofa and hid from the commotion.

"What's going on?" Lofton asked, then followed the three girls into Holly's bedroom. "I thought ya'll had plans to go to Ponce to shop tonight."

Holly said, "Not anymore. I've got to get on a plane to New York."

Stella turned to Lofton and explained everything they knew about Marla's situation so far.

"Oh my gosh," Lofton said. "How can I help? Do you already have a ticket for your flight? Do you need a ride to the airport?"

"She does have a ticket," Kali answered. "Wagner got them. He's coming to pick her up in a few minutes, and they are flying to New York together. Someone from Garrison's PR team is taking Marla to the hospital now and will let Holly know more details soon."

Holly was standing in front of her closet scanning her clothes. Stella had already pulled Holly's carry-on out and had it open on her bed.

"What should I bring?" asked Holly. I don't know what to wear. What if I really am going to be on TV tomorrow morning? I don't feel prepared for that."

"I've got a great new blue dress," Lofton said. She left the room and went to get it.

Stella began going through Holly's closet and pulling dresses out, taking them off the hangers and putting them into the suitcase. "Holly," Stella said, "go pack up your makeup and other things you need. Lofton and I have your clothes."

Holly nodded. Kali followed Holly into the bathroom to help her gather her things. Lofton came back into Holly's room with a navy-blue dress and handed it to Stella to put into Holly's bag.

Kali's phone buzzed with a text. She pulled it from her pocket and told Holly, "Wagner is leaving his place in about ten minutes." Then she continued to help gather Holly's things from the bathroom.

Lofton poked her head into the bathroom. "There's nothing too large in that bag that won't go through security, is there?" she asked.

Kali and Holly shook their heads. "No, only travel-sized shampoo and stuff," Holly said.

"What about shoes?" Stella asked.

Holly went to her closet, pulled two pairs of heels in two different colors, and tossed those in. Then she added a pair of jeans, a sweatshirt, a sports bra, and a pair of old sorority knit shorts to sleep in. Finally, she put in her toiletries bag and zipped her carry-on closed.

"I think I have everything," Holly said. She took her bag from the bed and carried it into the living room. "Wait. Where's my large tote? It has my laptop and stuff from the office."

"That's still in my car," Stella said then bolted from the apartment to grab it.

When Stella walked back inside with Holly's bag, Holly said, "Just got a text from Wagner; he's on his way here. Thank you, guys, for all of your help. I'll let you know what's going on as soon as I can."

"Yeah, let us know," Stella said, then she hugged Holly. The four of them walked outside to wait in the parking lot for Wagner. Within a few minutes, they saw him driving up. Holly turned to Stella, Lofton, and Kali and said, "Romantic dinner plans are off the agenda, or so it seems."

"Maybe a romantic snack on the plane?" Stella suggested.

"But anything can happen in twenty-four hours, especially in New York City," Lofton said with a grin.

29
A Night to Remember

Holly and Wagner both had PreCheck and made it through security quickly, getting to their gate just as their plane was starting to board. Their seats, unfortunately, weren't together, but at least Wagner managed to put Holly's carry-on in a space above his seat, which was several rows in front of hers. He only had his messenger bag and a backpack, and he stored those under the seat in front of him. When Holly made it to her seat, she placed her large tote in front of her feet, clicked her seatbelt, and began to worry about the situation that lay ahead of her. If she really were to take Marla's place on the show, would she come across as polished and professional as her boss? Would she get stage fright? But as the plane took off, she leaned her head back, closed her eyes, and remembered how easygoing and welcoming Bradley had been when they'd first met, and that made her feel a little better.

By the time they landed, and Holly turned her phone's Wi-Fi back on, she had a text from Garrison.

> Marla has been taken to East Elmhurst Hospital. Michael has been keeping me informed. He told me if she's admitted he would let me know. This is all I know for now.

The text had come in just over an hour ago. As the travelers around her began to deplane, she watched Wagner take her bag from the overhead compartment. He turned around, and their eyes met. Holly smiled and mouthed, "Thank you." When she met up with him at the gate, she shared the new information.

"She may have been admitted by now," Holly said to Wagner. "Should we go to the hospital?"

"Do you have Michael's cell?" Wagner asked.

Holly shook her head. "No. I'll ask Garrison to give it to me. That way he doesn't have to keep texting me information. I'll tell Garrison we are on our way to the hospital."

Wagner looked at Holly and nodded. "That sounds like a good idea."

"Okay," Holly said, texting Garrison, who got back to her right away. "I have Michael's number," she told Wagner. "I'll text him and tell him we are on our way to the hospital now."

Wagner said, "Good," then he pulled the Uber app up on his phone. He and Holly walked through the airport exit and began making their way down the sidewalk toward the Uber pick-up spot to wait.

After their driver dropped them off in front of the emergency-room doors, Holly had still not heard back from Michael.

"Michael still hasn't texted me back. I'll try calling him." Holly said.

"Hello," Michael answered.

"Michael. It's Holly. I'm here in the emergency room. Wagner and I just got here. How is Marla?"

"She's just come back from imaging. And they've decided that the pain she is feeling in her stomach is from appendicitis. She is going to be prepped for surgery soon. I'm with her now. After they take her to surgery, I'll come down to the waiting room."

Holly and Wagner went into the emergency waiting room. Holly wheeled her carry-on bag over to two empty chairs and sat in one.

"I'll text Stella and Kali and let them know to tell Joe everything that's going on," Holly said.

"I texted Joe after we got on the plane. I'll continue to keep him up-to-date." Wagner said. "Since it sounds like Marla is going to have surgery, should someone contact Bradley's staff to let her know that you will be doing the interview instead?"

"Yeah, I should see if Garrison is handling that."

Holly started sending updates on Marla to both Stella and Garrison. Wagner pulled a paperback out of his bag and started reading. Holly glanced at the title of Wagner's book, curious to know his reading taste. It was a worn-looking paperback copy of *One Hundred Years of Solitude* by Gabriel Garcia Marquez. Holly had heard of the book and thought that it might have won awards, but she had never read it. After sending her texts, she turned to Wagner and asked him what the book was about, because she wanted to learn more about the things that interested him.

Wagner let out a short laugh. He held his paperback up so that Holly could see the cover. "I read it in high school. And it was a tough read back then. Honestly, while I was packing earlier, I grabbed the first book I could from my bookshelf and tossed it into my bag. Just in case I wanted to read on the plane or if I found I had some time on my hands, you know?" He smiled at Holly, and his eyes searched hers. "I didn't even realize which book I'd picked up."

"I've never read it," Holly said. "Did the book win an award?"

Wagner shook his head. "No, but the author did win the Nobel Prize in Literature. It's a hard book to understand. There are a lot of characters, and topics to keep up with. The story spans a great length of time, and the author paints a picture of family life that moves through many generations. Over the years, the family is unable to break some of their repeated patterns, mistakes, and such. And decisions made by earlier generations continue to affect the family. There are some magical and supernatural elements within the story too. The book sheds light on political issues in South America. Some things might even get lost a bit within the English translation. But mainly what I remember from reading it in high school was that the author taps deeply into human emotion. And it seemed to me that there was one thing that kept haunting the family through the generations, and it was also the reason they did the things that they did—and that was their profound sense of solitude. It continued to haunt them."

Wagner closed the book. "By reading it a second time, I have a feeling that I will get something totally different out of the story. It's just the kind of book it is. It's not a comfort-read, like I feel the Harry Potter books are for me. This is an educational and a thought-provoking read, definitely not light reading."

Holly nodded. She was impressed yet again by something Wagner had explained. He was so smart, and she felt she might be a little out of his league, or was he out of her league; was it an "opposites-attract" type of thing? But as long as they got along and had things in common, then maybe the fact he was smarter than she was didn't matter. Besides, they seemed to have the same sense of humor, and both enjoyed watching *The Office*. And once she'd started paying closer attention to Wagner, she'd felt an attraction, there was chemistry between them. She moved in her chair and swiveled her knees to face him. When she did, her knee touched his, and tingles moved across her skin.

"I really like Harry Potter too," Holly said. "But I guess I'm not much into reading classics."

"Yeah," Wagner said with a chuckle. "It's kinda funny that this was the book I grabbed without looking."

Just then Michael walked into the waiting room. Holly spotted him first and called him over. Michael looked exhausted, like he'd been up all night covering the news in a war zone, but Holly had just seen him at the office earlier that afternoon. He had shed his navy sport coat and the sleeves of his white button-down shirt were rolled up to his elbows. He was carrying Marla's large tote bag with him, the one that had the *Beyond* magazine logo on one side.

"How is she?" Holly said as she stood up.

"They just wheeled her away for surgery," Michael said and sat down next to Wagner. "I'm glad you were able to get here," he said looking at Holly. "That's all Marla kept talking about, even though she was in a lot of pain. She kept telling me to make sure Garrison was able to get you on the show with Bradley tomorrow morning as her replacement. I think Garrison has already handled the details on that. At least he said he was going to. He will probably call you. And she wanted to give you these. She said they were to give to Bradley and her staff, I think." He pulled copies of the summer issue from the tote bag.

Holly said, "Okay." She went over and took the magazines from him. "Do you know how long Marla will be in surgery?"

"They didn't really say. I don't know. Maybe they said an hour in surgery." Michael put his head down and settled it in his hands, with his elbows resting on his knees. "There is another waiting room on the floor where she's having surgery, and I'll go back up there soon." With his head still down, Michael looked as if he was speaking to the floor. Then he looked back up. "I appreciate you guys coming here. But don't feel like you need to hang around the hospital. You should at least try to get some sleep. Garrison handled our hotel room for this trip, and I had him cancel it for me. I'm not going anywhere. The hospital is holding our suitcases somewhere for us."

Holly and Wagner both nodded. Holly leaned over and gave Michael's arm a squeeze. "I'm sorry, Michael," she said.

Just then Garrison walked into the waiting room and saw Holly. "Holly!" he said as he jogged toward her. He reached for her arm and pulled her aside. "Can I speak with you?" he asked.

Holly said yes, and the two of them moved into a far corner of the room. Wagner had started talking to Michael about Marla, and Holly glanced at Wagner while Garrison rattled off information to her.

"Bradley's staff and producers have been notified that Marla was taken to the hospital tonight for emergency surgery," he said. "I've given them the name of the hospital, and they know what is going on. I've also let them know that you are here and will be filling in tomorrow for Marla. I can have a car come to pick you up in the morning at seven thirty. Once you arrive at the studio, they will work on your hair and makeup, and your breakfast will be provided by craft services. You will be the first guest. Before you go on, someone from the studio will go over everything with you, and they will explain what questions Bradley might ask you and things like that. You will be able to ask questions too. The show ends at noon, but stick around for photos and press afterward. Let me know where you're staying, and I'll have my driver pick you up in the morning."

Holly stared at Garrison for a beat. She didn't know where she'd be staying. She and Wagner had just gotten to the hospital without a thought about much else. "Uh," she said and looked around for Wagner. She saw that Michael was still sitting in the chair with his head down, but she didn't see Wagner anywhere.

"I'll need to get back to you on where I'm staying," she replied. "Sorry, Garrison. It's just been a lot, you know?"

Garrison nodded. "Sure. You can get back to me on that. I should have kept the hotel room that Michael had me cancel. Neither of us is thinking straight right now. I'm just glad you were able to be here for Marla." His features held a look of sincerity.

"I am too," Holly said, then she turned to walk back toward Michael. Garrison started to follow her, then grabbed her arm to get her attention. "There's something else," he said. "I wanted to tell you I'm sorry for . . . you know. I know I sent flowers, but it means more for me to tell you in person. What you told me made sense, and it got me thinking. I don't want to come across as an insensitive, thoughtless jerk, caveman, asshole, whatever you want to call it."

Holly nodded. "Thank you, Garrison. I appreciate your apology. But I also want you to know it doesn't change how I feel. Sometimes you get a second chance, and that evening here in New York felt like a second chance with the guy I thought had gotten away. It just wasn't the second chance I was hoping for."

A look of sorrow filled his eyes. "I know," he said. "I screwed up twice with you, once in high school and again that night here in New York."

"I don't think you need to think about it as a missed opportunity or a screwup as much as a wake-up call to do things differently the next time," Holly told him. "Think of it as an opportunity to change the way you treat women in general. I heard from someone older and wiser once that you should *be* the person you are looking for is looking for, and incorporate all of those values, details, and beliefs into what that encompasses along with the way you interact with others."

"Yeah." He nodded. "Right. Well, I, uh, should . . . um . . . I'm gonna go and speak with Michael and see how he's holding up. I'll see you later. Um, thanks, Holly. And, again, for what it's worth, I truly am sorry that I blew it with you. I think you are a great person. It's my loss."

They both walked over to where Michael was still sitting with his head in his hands. Garrison sat in the seat next to Michael. Holly put a hand on Michael's shoulder.

"Where is Wagner?" Holly asked.

Michael looked up at her. "He said he needed some air. Maybe he went outside."

Holly walked quickly through the emergency-room doors, her eyes darting back and forth to scan the area beneath the portico. She started to feel panic creeping in. Did Wagner think Garrison was there to see her? Did he think there was something going on between her and him? Did he think she was interested in him? Had Wagner put bits and pieces together from the office conversations he'd overheard between her and Stella—and come up with his own ideas about her relationship with Garrison? She walked out onto the sidewalk and continued to look around. Then she spotted Wagner sitting on a bench along the sidewalk with his bags next to him. She made her way over to him.

"Wagner," she called.

He looked up at her.

"Are you okay?" she asked.

He nodded. "Yeah, just needed some air. Came out here to clear my head."

Holly sat down on the bench next to him.

"I wanted to make sure I gave you some privacy," he said. "Uh, if you needed to speak with Garrison about something other than work, I mean."

"Huh?" Holly looked concerned and a little worried. "No. I don't want you to get the wrong idea."

Holly looked into Wagner's eyes, and they held each other's gaze as her eyes searched his. Maybe Wagner had even picked up on the fact that she'd not been clear about who had sent the tulips, and perhaps he now understood who they were really from—he was smart after all. Maybe he really thought there was something going on between her and Garrison. Or that there had been something between them in the past and Garrison was trying hard to win her back.

"Wagner, Garrison was just explaining what would happen in the morning. He's going to send a car to take me or us——"she waved a finger between herself and Wagner—"to the studio. He gave me the details and even asked where I was staying so he could send a car. I guess we need to find a hotel." She hesitated for a beat, still holding his gaze. Then she reached out and placed her hand on top of his. "I hope you don't think there's anything to what Stella said earlier today when the call came in from Garrison to me. Because there is absolutely nothing between me and Garrison Simmons."

Wagner's eyes filled with a look of relief. He lifted his face, and a smile began to form on his lips. He placed his other hand on top of hers, then he said, "I'm from here. My parents have a place on the Upper East Side. They are still at their home in Florida and won't be back for a few more days. I'll call us an Uber."

"Oh, well, in that case, I'll go back and let Michael know that we are leaving. I'll get my suitcase, and I'll also need to give Garrison your address."

30

Twenty-Four Hours in NYC: Yes, Please!

By the time the Uber driver pulled up to the address that Wagner had given him, it was almost three a.m. When Holly and Wagner stepped out onto the sidewalk, Holly looked up to see the name of the building, which was called The Fairmont. A bellman opened the door for them, and they walked across a marble-floored foyer toward a bay of elevators. Wagner pulled out a keycard, held it in front of the elevator, and pushed a button. The elevator doors opened, and he stepped inside, Holly followed.

If Holly had not been so tired, she might have asked more questions about Wagner's family, how long he had lived in New York, what it was like to go to boarding school, and maybe even what his parents did for a living. As the elevator began to rise, she thought if she were to mention boarding school, he'd know she'd read his bio. But then again, it was on their website for everyone to see anyway. Instead, she giggled, the exhaustion taking over, and asked, "Do your parents know you're bringing a girl home to spend the night?"

Wagner looked down at her and smiled. A curl had escaped from his somewhat unruly mop of brown waves. It flopped over his left eye, and he didn't bother to brush it away.

"Yes, actually they do know. I called them when I left work today to tell them about the situation and that I'd be coming home and bringing someone with me. They were excited but also disappointed since they aren't planning to fly home from Florida until Monday evening."

The elevator doors opened onto a hallway. Wagner walked toward a doorway, and again used his keycard, which unlocked the front door. They stepped into a beautiful, glossy foyer, where a round antique table with curved legs held an enormous floral arrangement. The scent of the flowers rose up to greet them in a most pleasant way. As she passed the table, Holly saw an office on one side and the kitchen up ahead. On the other side was a large, open living space, and a wall of windows glowed with the New York skyline.

"It's stunning, so beautiful," Holly said, almost in a whisper. She stood still, mesmerized by millions of lights from the city that never sleeps.

"The view is very beautiful," Wagner agreed. But was he talking about the skyline, which he'd seen a bazillion times, or was he talking about the girl standing in front of the windows? He extended his hand in front of him, then said, "Here. Let me show you which room you'll be staying in. This way."

As they moved through the living area, they passed an extremely large leather sectional. Another tall, elegant bouquet of flowers sat on another exquisite antique table. Holly breathed in the sweet aroma as she followed Wagner.

"These floral arrangements are massive and stunning, but if there's no one else here, who would be around to enjoy them?" she asked. She felt bad almost right away for asking such an odd question.

"Mom has them scheduled to be replaced once a week. I guess sometimes they even come when they are out of town. They'll be back in a few days, and since these look fresh, I'm sure they'll be just as lovely when Mom and Dad return."

They passed the kitchen and entered a long hallway. Holly scanned her surroundings as if she were a pauper in a palace. Wagner stopped at a doorway, then stepped into the room. "This was my younger sister's room at one time," he said. "She's hardly ever here anymore. She's a senior at Chapman in California." He grinned. "We'll, I guess technically I'm not here much anymore either."

Holly pulled her carry-on bag into the room, her feet sinking into the thick carpet. She could not wait to get her shoes off. The room was painted the palest shade of pink. A king-sized bed took up most of one wall. Another wall held two large windows with built-in seats topped with a variety of light pink and white cushions and pillows. The window seating had long, thick floral-print curtains on either side, held open by thick tassels to reveal more nighttime views of the city. The wall opposite the bed had two large wooden doors spaced evenly apart. Wagner walked over and opened one door. "This is the closet. If there's anything in there you need, just help yourself."

Holly walked over and peeked inside. It was huge, at least ten feet in length and five feet wide. The sides were lined with floor-to-ceiling shelving and hanging space. In the middle was a narrow island with cubbies full of handbags. Small drawers lined the edges of the island.

"Wow," Holly said. "I'd love a closet like this. I think it would make it easier to figure out what to wear."

Wagner laughed a little. "I guess," he said. "The other door is the bathroom."

They walked out of the closet, and she followed him over to the other door. The bathroom was huge too. It had both a shower and a clawfoot tub. Holly said she wished she had time to soak in the tub, and Wagner blushed.

"There are towels and shampoo and everything you need in the closet." Wagner opened a tall, thin linen closet inside the bathroom. Sure enough, the shelves held shampoo, soap, toilet paper, towels, and even a hairdryer and a few curling irons. Everything looked perfect with each item having its own spot; nothing seemed out of place, but if Holly had not been so tired, she might have felt a little weird about being there.

"My room is down the hall on the left," Wagner said. "If you need anything or whatever, just, um, knock."

"How far down the hall on the left are you?" Holly asked. "Just wondering in case, I get spooked or something." Holly giggled a little to show she was only playing with him.

Wagner grinned a little then said, "It's the only door down the hall on the left. There's another room down on the right, but it's a guest room, and it might be filled with boxes, not sure. No one goes in there or uses that room. The bed might not even be made."

"Okay," Holly said. "Just want to be sure. And your parent's room is . . .?"

"On the opposite hallway. It's on the other side of the kitchen. And there's a workout room over on that hallway too. In case you feel the need to lift a few weights while you're here."

They both chuckled a little.

Holly moved out of the bathroom. "I'm definitely too tired for anything right now except sleep. We only have a few hours before we need to be up to get ready to go to the studio. Thank you for bringing me here. Your home is so lovely. Everything is so elegant and beautiful."

Wagner walked close to Holly. He looked down at her, and his eyes twinkled. "I'm glad you are here. And I wouldn't want to be anywhere else right now," he said. "Good night, Holly. Sleep well. I guess I'll see you around seven . . . uh, in a few hours."

The way he was looking at her made heat rush to her cheeks. His voice was soft and comforting, like a warm blanket that she wanted to curl up into. Her mouth felt dry, and her throat felt thick. With her lips parted, she breathed through her mouth for a beat, then said, "Good night, Wagner."

He walked across the room to the door, grabbed the knob, stepped into the hallway, and slowly pulled the door closed, keeping his eyes on Holly the whole time as if he were trying to memorize every inch of her. Right before he closed the door, he whispered, "Good night."

Holly walked over to the closed door, leaned against it, and thought, *I wish he'd kissed me.*

31

In a New York Minute

When Holly's phone buzzed her awake, it was six forty-five, and it felt as if she'd only slept for thirty minutes. She slid out from under the thick blankets and soft sheets and made her way into the bathroom to shower and wash her hair. The last thing she'd done right before she'd gone to bed was to hang up the dress she was going to take to wear on the show, and she'd found a travel hanging bag inside Wagner's sister's closet to put her dress and shoes in. She was thankful that the studio would be doing her hair and makeup.

By the time she got out of the shower, she had a text from Garrison saying he was sending a car her way. Quickly, she put on a more casual dress. Then she made her way out of the bathroom with the hanging bag in one hand and her large tote in the other. When she got down the hall and looked toward the kitchen, she could see Wagner standing next to the long marble island sipping a cup of coffee. A travel mug sat next to him on the counter. She walked into the kitchen, and he looked up and smiled.

"I made you a cup of coffee," he said.

"Thank you," she said and set her tote down before taking the travel mug from him. "I got a text from Garrison. He's sending a car, so I guess we should go downstairs."

Wagner nodded. "Do you have everything you need?"

"Yes. They're going to fix my hair and makeup on set," Holly said, thinking maybe Wagner was wondering about her lack of put-togetherness.

Wagner picked up Holly's large tote, and together they made their way out the door.

"Have you heard anything from Michael this morning?" she asked on their way to the elevator.

"Not yet. I thought I'd try to get ahold of him once we're at the studio. I'll have plenty of time to talk to Michael after we get there. I'm sure he had a rough night and not much sleep either."

After they walked out to the sidewalk, it wasn't long before Garrison texted that a black town car would be arriving shortly. Soon, one pulled up, and Holly recognized Rick, who'd picked her and Garrison up at Sardi's. Rick greeted them with a friendly good morning as they stepped into the back seat. As they got on their way, the traffic was as crazy as ever, but Wagner seemed unfazed by the horns and sudden stops. Holly sent a group text to Stella, Kali, and Lofton, letting them know she and Wagner had seen Michael before Marla's surgery but didn't have any more news. She told them she was on the way to the ABC studios and to wish her luck so that she wouldn't sound like a total dork on TV.

The driver let them out in front of 77 West Sixty-Sixth Street, and Wagner and Holly went into the foyer, followed the signs to the elevators, and rode up to the floor where they'd been told to go. When they arrived, a man wearing a shirt with the show's name and logo greeted them and showed them to a dressing room. As they walked into the room, he asked them what they'd like to eat, naming a few items. Holly and Wagner told him what they'd like, and the man said he'd have someone bring those in a few minutes. Before he left, he said, "Someone from makeup will be in shortly."

In the dressing room, a tall director's chair was placed in front of a large makeup mirror with a couch and coffee table arranged against a wall. Wagner took a seat on the couch, and within a few minutes a girl came to the door with the food and drinks Holly and Wagner had requested and set the tray on the coffee table. Wagner handed Holly one of the cups of coffee, then he sat down, and picked up one of the donuts, and took a bite. Holly reached for the toast with grape jelly and nibbled a little before sitting next to Wagner. Together they sat quietly for a few moments eating their breakfast until another knock came. Holly got up to answer the door for the tall makeup artist. "I'm Ginger," she said. "Are you ready for makeup?" Holly nodded, brushed the crumbs off her hands, and took a seat in the director's chair in front of the mirror.

As Ginger worked on Holly, Wagner stretched out on the couch with his feet propped up, and Holly thought he'd fallen asleep because he was so quiet. Since she was facing the mirror and chatting with the makeup artist, she couldn't see Wagner, but she might have heard a snore. Before the makeup artist was completely finished, the hairstylist came by to take a look and asked how she normally wore her hair. Since it was already a little curly, he decided to dry it with a diffuser and add a few more beachy waves to her already tumble-tossed curls. After he was done, Holly and Wagner were once again alone. Holly wondered about getting dressed. She would need Wagner to leave the room so she could change. Would it be awkward for her to ask him? Or awkward to wake him up? Or both? Or should she just change really quickly, and maybe he wouldn't notice?

She started to take her things out of the bag. She hung the dress on a hook on the wall and took off her Golden Goose tennis shoes. She tucked her socks into her shoes and decided to wake Wagner. She stood over him and leaned down. "Wagner," she whispered.

His eyes fluttered open, and he smiled when he saw her. "Hey," he said. His voice sounded heavy and sleepy. "Are you about to go on?"

"No, I just need to change into my dress."

"Oh," he said and sat up.

He wasn't really moving to leave the room, so Holly said, "I'm changing in here if you don't mind stepping outside for a minute."

"Right. Sorry," he said. "You look beautiful by the way," he added as he stepped into the hallway.

"You haven't seen the full picture yet," Holly said just as Wagner shut the door.

Holly had chosen to wear Lofton's new navy-blue dress. It was long sleeved and low-cut, with a gathered knot to one side at her waist and a split that showed most of her right leg. It flattered her figure perfectly. Her hips looked full, the dress narrowed her waist, and the deep V-neck showed just a little bit of cleavage. She slipped off her bra and opened the package that contained a flesh-colored adhesive, strapless bra and she secured the cups into place. She'd brought taupe strappy heels to complete the outfit. When she had finished changing, she opened the door. Wagner, who had apparently been texting with someone, turned around, and the look he gave her was priceless. "You . . . you," he stammered. "You look breathtaking, Holly," he finally managed to get out.

"Thank you." She did a twirl. She felt elegant but also a little like a rock star.

Wagner stepped back into the dressing room, and Holly closed the door. Together they sat down on the couch, but as soon as they did, there was a knock on the door.

"Holly Curtis," someone called.

Holly got up and opened the door. Standing in the hallway was a staff member wearing headphones with some rolled-up papers in his hand.

"I'm Jonathan," he said. "I'm going to go over the questions that Bradley will be asking you today. Can I come in?"

"Yes." Holly opened the door wider to let Jonathan inside.

"So, there's going to be an introduction about *Beyond* magazine, and we pulled your bio from the website." He unrolled the papers, chose the one he wanted her to look at, and handed it over for her to read. Then he rolled the other papers back up and stuck the roll into his back pocket. "Is there anything that you would like to add to this?"

"No, it's fine the way it is," Holly said after taking a brief look.

"Those introductions are your cue to walk out. So step onto the set just after your name is mentioned."

Jonathan took the paper from Holly and produced a new one from his back pocket for her to look at. "These are the questions that Bradley will be asking about the magazine specifically, and all of this will be on the prompter. So you'll be able to see what questions are coming next before she asks them. You can read over these now. Do you have any questions for me?"

Holly scanned the page, then she looked up at him and said, "I don't think so."

"Okay. I'll leave that page with you." He rolled up the other paper and stuck it into his back pocket. Then he pulled a communication device from his hip and said, "One, one all clear, it's a go." He clipped the radio back to its holster and told Holly, "When it's fifteen minutes till showtime, someone will knock on the door to let you know it's time. At that point, you and your friend . . ." Jonathan looked over at Wagner. "You both will be taken backstage, and after you hear the introduction about Beyond then your name, you'll walk onto the set and sit on the couch. And if you've ever seen Bradley's show, you already know where to sit."

Holly nodded. "I have. So, do I wave to the crowd as I'm walking out?"

"Yes, that would be perfect. You will be a natural. After the show is over, there will be photos with Bradley in our greenroom. Someone will take you there, then you are free to go. Can you think of anything else?"

Holly nodded and turned around, went to her tote, and pulled out three copies of *Beyond*. "I've got a few copies of the magazine with me if you or Bradley would like one."

"Thank you for the reminder." He took the magazines from Holly. "I'll have someone from props set these out on set. I know this might be your first time on TV, but try not to let your nerves get to you."

Holly nodded. "Great advice."

32
Lights, Camera, Action

The lights were really bright when Holly walked onto the stage. Bradley rose from her seat and hugged Holly with a friendly greeting. She had just given *Beyond* a great plug, introducing it as one of the most dynamic and thought-provoking magazines for women, about women. She'd held up the summer issue for the audience to see. And there was a stack of five more on the table in front of her. After Bradley's glowing introduction of *Beyond,* she'd introduced Holly, then asked if Holly would like to give away some copies of the magazine to a few lucky audience members.

Holly picked up two of the copies and walked toward a lady who was jumping up and down in excitement, eager to be picked. Then she walked to the opposite side of the stage and handed out another copy. Bradley, in the meantime, was telling everyone else to go buy one as soon as they left the studio.

After Holly sat back down, Bradley told the audience about how Marla had gotten the idea to start *Beyond*, mentioning that Marla had had emergency surgery earlier that morning. Bradley then switched gears and asked Holly when she first knew she wanted to work for a magazine. And she was curious to hear what Holly thought was the best part about working for *Beyond*.

"Working for *Beyond* magazine has been the fulfillment of a longtime dream for me," Holly began. She looked out into the audience. "Or at least it feels that way. I've only been out of college for about two years. So talking about lifetime dreams being fulfilled in a short period of time is cool, but I know living out a lifetime of dreams or achievements will be a long time coming. And I'm here for it." She gave a short laugh. "I don't think we should ever give up on our dreams or on turning those into reality. And it's so incredible to be a part of searching out and telling inspirational stories about women from all over the world. I've learned so many things about other cultures from some of the interviews I've done. Each day, we not only find new things in and around the city of Atlanta to write about, but we also look for stories about women that might get overlooked, and we bring those into the light. I think sometimes the hardest part is picking just one cover story. We want to feature women, like Bradley Banner, who are leaving their marks on their communities," she said to the audience. "Women who are making changes, and implementing new ideas, striving to go beyond—pun intended, of course."

The audience laughed. Then Bradley said, "I'm grateful to be your cover story for the summer issue. It is an honor, especially knowing that you search the world over to find women who have unique stories to tell. So to have been chosen by your editor in chief means a great deal to me personally. Tell us what the future holds for *Beyond*."

"Right now, we are looking to expand our readership into the Midwest and far western states. We already have the Southeastern states covered. And, Bradley, since you're on our cover, we've gotten into a few Manhattan locations. Our plan is to continue to grow our readership, expand, and hopefully become a nationwide magazine. And after that we'd love to find distribution in other parts of the world. Because we interview women all over the world, maybe Beyond will have offices one day in Europe and in Asia too."

Bradley nodded. "Yes," she said. "What a dream come true that would be. But that's what is so inspiring about your company, Holly. *Beyond*, was the dream child of its editor, Marla Monroe, only three years ago. A company she started from scratch—straight out of college and with hard work and determination—is already growing by leaps and bounds, and it has potential that is undeniable."

"Right," Holly said. "And we work with a small crew of only six people now, but that's changing. We have a few new recruits who are graduating in a few weeks and who will start working for *Beyond* next month."

"What advice do you have for any of those who might be watching right now who have an interest in writing for a magazine or working in that field?"

Holly smiled at Bradley. "Great question. I'd tell them to work toward a degree in journalism and maybe get a minor in media studies or marketing. Start your own blog, create a unique and positive social-media platform—maybe even a podcast—and always be on the lookout for interesting people or subjects to talk about or interview."

"Wonderful advice, Holly. We thank you for being with us and for sharing a little about what it's like to work for a female-centered magazine and blog. Holly Curtis, everyone—cover-story writer and journalist for *Beyond*." Applause broke out throughout the crowd.

"Before we head into a commercial break," Bradley told the audience, "we have joining us today some models from Macy's department store showing off some summer fashion trends and hot colors in everything from dresses to shorts to swimwear. And our studio audience will be going home with fifty-dollar Macy's gift cards. Everyone, take a look underneath your seats!"

As the excited audience began to bustle about in their seats, Bradley stood and shook Holly's hand. Holly stood as well, and the women embraced just as the models took the stage.

33

I Love NYC

Once the show was over, Holly and Wagner were sent to the greenroom for promo and press photos with Bradley. Several were taken of just Holly and Bradley, some with the summer issue of *Beyond* in their hands. The crew even captured a few shots of Wagner with Bradley and Holly and a few of just Holly and Wagner. Wagner was quick to snap a few of Holly and Bradley for Beyond's social-media sites. A photographer from the studio told Holly they would email the crew's photos to her. They made their way back to the dressing room, where Holly gathered her bags and clothes. She decided she could change later and stayed in the interview dress.

As soon as they were on the elevator heading down to the street level, Holly asked if Wagner had heard anything from Michael about Marla.

"I texted him while you were changing. He just got back to me a few minutes ago. His latest text said that Marla had a hard time coming out of the anesthesia and they kept her in intensive care, but Michael thought the doctor should be making his rounds soon, and he was hoping she would get into a room. He's been up all night." He pulled out his phone. "I'll try to call him now," Wagner said. "What do you want to do? Go over to the hospital?"

"Sure," Holly said.

Holly pulled up her Uber app while Wagner called Michael.

"No answer," he said. "But we can go by the hospital and check to see if they've put her in a room. If they have, Michael might finally be sleeping."

Holly nodded, then told him the Uber was a gray Honda.

When they got into the back of the Uber, Holly noticed she had fifteen text messages. She started to read through them and texted replies to Stella and Lofton. Both of them had said she looked amazing on TV and had aced the interview. They were thrilled, they said, to have a famous friend. Holly scrolled through a few more texts, answering and commenting as she went. Then her phone rang, and she saw it was her mother. Holly gasped and almost dropped her phone.

She grabbed Wagner by the arm.

He turned to face her, alarmed by the look of sheer panic that covered her face.

"Holly, what's wrong?"

"My mother is calling me."

"Okay. Do you need to answer?"

"I forgot to tell her I was here in New York. Oh. My. God. Did she see me on TV?"

She glanced at her phone. "Voicemail. She left me a voicemail."

"I'm sure she'll understand," said Wagner. "It was a last-minute-emergency overnight kind of trip. Do you want to call her back?"

"I want to do literally *anything* but call her back."

Wagner laughed. "It's not that bad, is it?"

"You don't know my mother. She wants to be involved in everything. She still tracks my phone, then calls to ask me what I'm doing and who I'm with. She is always worried and wanting me to text her, especially when she knows I'm traveling. Okay, she might not track me all the time anymore, but she used to do it a lot. She thinks I keep things from her on purpose."

Wagner lifted an eyebrow. "You sound like my sister. She hated it when our mom got all up in her business. She's very independent like you, I suppose."

"I cannot listen to this voicemail right now. I just can't. It will probably kill the high I'm on. I don't want her to ruin my day and make me feel guilty over forgetting to call her— which I do a lot. Maybe I'll text her and act like I was at the hospital until the wee hours of the morning. Then I had to be at the studio early and just haven't had a chance to call to let her know what was going on."

"Sure, that kinda *is* what happened," Wagner said, smiling at her.

"You don't get it do you, Wagner? Having a mom who wants to literally know everything all of the time."

"Uh, I guess that's not so bad. She cares. She loves you."

"She's too nosy."

Wagner laughed. "Text your mom, Holly."

Holly rolled her eyes and sent a text that would hopefully explain the urgency of the situation, the reason she'd forgotten to tell her where she was, and why she'd been on TV, hopefully that would pull her mom out of freak-out mode. After sending the text, she listened to her mom's voicemail.

"Holly," her mom's message began, "I just got a call from Doris from my book club. She said she saw you on the *'In a New York Minute'* show with Bradley Banner. By the way, Doris said she went and bought a copy right after you were on the show. I had to lie and pretend that I knew all about it when, of course, I had no earthly idea what in the world she was talking about. Surely you've not gone back to New York City and been on a TV show without telling me or your father about what is going on. I just can't imagine. It is possible that Doris was hallucinating. She tends to be a real scatterbrain at times. But, nevertheless, you need to call your mother."

After getting to the hospital, they learned at the front desk that Marla had been put in room 211, so they headed to the elevator and up to the second floor, where they could hopefully see her. When they arrived outside the room, the door was slightly ajar. Holly knocked lightly, and she heard a faint voice say, "Come in."

They peeped in to find Marla awake with Michael sleeping in the chair next to her bed. Her face lit up when she saw Holly and Wagner.

"Oh, Holly. You look so beautiful. How did everything go?" Marla's voice was soft, and she sounded tired.

"I think it went well."

Holly and Wagner stepped quietly into the room.

"She did great," Wagner said.

"I only got to see the last few minutes of your interview," said Marla. "I had the nurse turn the TV on for me as soon as I got in here. But I knew you would be amazing."

"How are you doing?" Holly asked.

"I think I'm doing okay now. It was a little touch and go for a while. And poor Michael, he's had it rough. He's finally getting some sleep."

"Do you know when you will be released?"

"Not yet. My doctor came by and saw me a few minutes ago. He's the one who did my midnight surgery. Since I had a hard time coming out of the anesthesia, he stayed with me in intensive care until he felt I was out of the woods. I haven't been in this room very long. I'm hoping when he makes his rounds tomorrow, I'll find out when I can go."

A knock came at the door, and everyone turned to see the door open. A nurse walked in with a huge bouquet of flowers and a "Get Well" balloon that floated above them. She set them on the side table by Marla and handed her the card.

"They're from Bradley Banner," Marla said. "That's so nice of her."

Holly nodded. She and Wagner moved to stand near the foot of the bed. Another nurse came into the room with a tray of food. "Hello," she called, walking in. "You might not feel like eating yet. But I've brought you some soup and Jell-O. Try to eat a little." The nurse pulled out Marla's tray table and scooted it close to her. Then she said she would be back to check on her shortly.

Holly and Wagner talked to Marla about the whole experience at the studio, and in a few minutes another nurse came in with two more bouquets. Both were much smaller than the first.

"Holly, would you read the cards to me?" Marla asked.

Holly pulled the card from the first bouquet. "This one is from Garrison." Then she pulled the card from the second envelope. "Oh, and these are from Kali, Joe, Stella, me, and Wagner. How nice."

"Aww," Marla said. "Those are beautiful. Do you see my phone?"

Holly looked around the room and saw Marla's tote sitting on the counter across from the bed. She walked over and picked up the tote. "Maybe it's in here," she said. After looking through the bag, she pulled out Marla's cell phone. The huge number of messages on it seemed more overwhelming than the voicemail Holly had gotten from her mother. She handed it to Marla.

"Geez," Marla said. "I've got a lot of catching up to do, phone calls to make, and texts to send, but I've also got nothing better to do right now." She chuckled a little.

Holly looked at Wagner. "We should let you get some rest and eat a little lunch," she said. "But please call or text me if you need us to bring you anything—or to do anything for Michael after he wakes up. We'll be here in a heartbeat, Marla."

34

A Night Out or a Night In

As Holly and Wagner left the hospital, he asked if she'd like to take a walk through Central Park.

"That sounds so perfect," she said. "But to be honest, and I know this will sound pathetically boring, but I just want to go to bed. I am so tired. I want to change, get really comfortable, and sleep. Is that okay? Could we go back to your place?"

"Yes. I'm a little tired too," he said, and she thought she saw a look of relief pass across his face. Holly wondered if he was glad that she felt comfortable enough to ask to go back to his place and sleep.

On their ride to the Upper East Side and back to Wagner's, Holly finally called her mother and explained in detail everything that had happened in the last twenty-four hours. She wasn't sure, she said, when Marla would be released from the hospital. She wasn't even totally sure how long she'd be in New York. She told her mother that she was there with a co-worker. What she left out was that she was with a male co-worker who she most definitely had the hots for.

When they walked into Wagner's parents' apartment, Holly went into the room she was staying in, and she noticed the bed had been made.

"Wagner," she called from the doorway.

He came down the hall and stopped in front of her. "Need something?" he asked.

"Has someone been in to make my bed? Are they still here?"

Wagner shook his head. "My parents have someone who comes in every morning to clean, do a little laundry, and replace any groceries. I'm sure they asked her to stop by since I told them I'd be home for a few days."

"Oh. Is it okay if I take a bath and a nap?"

"Yes." He said it softly. "Relax. I want you to feel at home."

She loved the way he looked at her. A deep sense of desire seemed to fill his dark brown eyes as they took in every inch of her. It made her pulse race. A warmth rose to her cheeks, she felt flushed, and her stomach turned multiple flips.

"Thanks," she said quietly. "I guess I'll see you later then."

She closed the door, then went to draw her bath before getting in and taking a relaxing soak. After the hot bath, she wrapped a thick towel around herself and curled up in the large, comfortable bed and napped. Several hours later, she crawled out from under the luxurious-feeling sheets and padded across the room to put on her sweatshirt, shorts, and socks. Then she opened the door and stepped into the hallway. As an intoxicating aroma wafted through the air, she breathed it in, and felt her tummy rumble. She wondered if there was also a chef who came to the apartment to cook. When she walked into the kitchen, she saw Wagner at the stove, stirring a pot of something.

"Hey, Wagner," she said.

He turned around and smiled. "Sleep well?" he asked.

"I did. I think I'm fully refreshed. Or will be soon. Whatever you're making smells amazing."

She walked over to stand beside him. Next to Wagner on the counter were sliced lemons, freshly chopped parsley, a pile of grated Parmesan cheese, garlic, and a stick of butter. Wagner took some drained pasta noodles from a strainer and placed them into a skillet on the stove. He then poured some pasta water into the skillet, bathing the noodles with a small amount of water. From what Holly could tell, he'd already added chopped garlic and a slice of butter to the pan.

"It's almost ready," he said.

"What can I do?" Holly asked.

"Could you take the French bread out of the oven?"

"Okay," Holly said and looked around until she saw a pot holder. She picked it up and opened the door to the oven. Inside she found toasted slices of bread baking with butter bubbling on top. After she took the pan out of the oven, Wagner told her he'd set a plate for the bread on the counter. Holly got busy transferring the bread while Wagner finished tossing the pasta with fresh parsley, lemon, and shredded Parm.

"I've already set the table," Wagner said. His hands were full, so he jerked his head in the direction of the table, and Holly took the plate of bread and set it down in the center.

The table sat six but was set for two. Candles had already been lit, and there was a small bouquet of yellow tulips sitting in a crystal vase between the candles. Wagner plated the pasta, grabbed a pair of tongs, then set the plate next to the bread.

"Wine?" he asked.

"Yes, please."

"Red or white?" Wagner moved back into the kitchen and opened a small wine fridge.

"I love Moscato if you have that, or Prosecco."

Wagner nodded. "Whitney likes that. I bet we have Moscato."

Holly looked confused for a moment, then Wagner seemed to realize he'd never told Holly his sister's name. "Whitney is my sister. My parents probably keep a bottle for her just in case she decides to come home."

"What is she studying?"

"Film. She wants to be a producer, same as my dad. He's a film producer for movies. She thought about going to Belmont where I was getting my undergrad because she thought Nashville would be a cool town to live in. But after she was accepted into the film school at Chapman in California, that was it for her, no turning back."

"Oh," Holly said. She was starting to understand Wagner's background more. "I guess it was fun growing up with a dad in the film industry."

Wagner nodded then opened a drawer and pulled out a corkscrew. He opened a bottle of red wine then searched a cabinet for two wine glasses. Then he opened a bottle of Moscato and poured it into a glass for Holly. As he handed the glass to her, he said, "At times it was cool, especially on premiere nights. But he spent a lot of long hours working. He's mostly retired now, only consults on projects when asked. He and Mom really enjoy their time at their house in Florida these days."

He turned around and poured red wine into his own glass, then turned back to Holly and tapped his glass to hers.

"To you," he said.

"To you," she said back to him.

"To us," he said.

Holly giggled.

Wagner's face lit up. "To the dinner we finally get to enjoy, *and* on the same night we'd planned to have it."

Holly tapped her glass to Wagner's again and said, "Cheers to that."

"Shall we eat?" Wagner waved a hand in front of him. Holly walked toward the table and set her wine glass down.

"Did you get any sleep?" she asked.

Wagner nodded. He pulled out Holly's chair. "Almost two hours. I wanted to make sure I could fix dinner for you tonight with enough time to run to the store down the street for anything I needed. Turns out we had almost everything except popcorn, slice-and-bake cookies, salad, and, of course, flowers. I tried to get the ones I thought were your favorite. I decided to forgo the garden-salad ingredients for time's sake."

"Everything is perfect," Holly said. "It smells incredible. If that's any indication of how good it is, then I'll be waddling out of here."

Wagner snickered. "Mmm. I'll take that as a compliment."

After she was seated, Wagner turned off the kitchen lights then sat down. The table glowed in the light of the candles. He lifted the pasta plate and offered some to Holly before plating his own food.

"I read up on you a little," Holly said.

"Huh?" Wagner looked amused but also a little confused.

"Your bio on the Beyond website," Holly clarified. "I'd never read anyone's bio. Stella and I pulled it up yesterday. I was curious, after all, about who I'd be dining with tonight."

Her voice sounded seductive and playful. "I didn't know you were working toward a master's degree in audio engineering, or that you went to boarding school."

Wagner put his fork down. "Mm-hmm," he said. "The reason I'm in Atlanta is because I received a fellowship and a scholarship to attend Georgia Tech for grad school. And my roommate from Belmont, he got a scholarship to Georgia Tech for grad school too. Although, he's finished his master's and has taken a job in Washington state. I'm still plugging along. But, unlike me, he didn't start working a full-time job at a magazine while he was still in school. I'm in night classes now. Twice a week in the evenings, but I'm almost finished."

Holly took in all of this information. The more she learned about him, the more there was to like about him. Wagner was perfection—absolute chocolate-man perfection. She thought of the half-naked Valentine's chocolate men she'd seen for sale in cellophane-covered boxes. How had she ever snubbed this guy?

Holly sipped more of her wine. Wagner finished the last drop from his glass and got up to get the bottles. He refilled Holly's glass and then his own.

"And yes," he said. "I went to a boarding school in New Jersey from ninth through twelfth grades. My sister did too. She was a freshman when I was a senior there. It was a great school; I made a lot of friends and really found my place. Both my sister and I were involved with the theater productions there. I was even prefect for my house. After everybody gets to campus, there's a ceremony and you're sorted into houses like in Harry Potter."

"That's cool."

Wagner wiped the corner of his mouth with his napkin. "It's cool that you were curious enough about me to look me up. By the way, I did the same, but I looked you up a whole lot sooner, like the day I first met you. I wanted to know who the bubbly blonde with the amazing eyes and smile was."

Holly blushed. Her stomach did a tumble, and heat rushed through her body. His eyes, his smile, the way he looked at her made her feel known, sexy, and beautiful all at the same time.

They finished their meal and moved to the sink to wash dishes and load the dishwasher. His nearness was like a rush of adrenaline through her veins. Every once in a while, she'd move to place something in the dishwasher, and their hands or hips would touch. Those involuntary touches sent a flood of want through her body, making her woozy and taking her breath away.

Wagner turned on the dishwasher, then folded the towel he was holding and set it next to the sink.

"Popcorn or cookies?" he asked.

"Popcorn, please."

"Coming right up," he said. He looked at Holly, gave her a playful grin, then added, "Unless you'd prefer to go out for a night on the town instead of staying in on the couch with me?"

"No. Staying in sounds perfect."

35

You Color My World

After the popcorn was done, Wagner poured it into a large bowl and filled their wine glasses again. He asked Holly to carry the popcorn to the couch. She picked up the bowl and her wine glass and made her way over. Wagner walked over to the kitchen table, blew out one of the candles, and took it to the TV area along with the small vase of tulips. Then he got his wine glass and sat next to Holly on the couch.

"I wanted to keep the ambiance going," he said. He opened a drawer inside the coffee table and pulled out a lighter. He lit the candle and smiled at Holly.

Holly set the bowl of popcorn on the couch between them.

"There's a blanket behind you if you want it," Wagner said.

Holly turned around to grab the thick, fluffy leopard-print blanket, then pulled it across her knees. Wagner turned on the TV and found *The Office*. "Which season is your favorite?" he asked.

"Season four," she said.

He pulled his lips in, like he was trying not to smile, but soon a grin broke out. He dragged a hand through his curls, then turned to Holly and said, "Same."

Their eyes met. Holly moved a little closer to Wagner. Their shoulders were almost touching, and the popcorn bowl was the only thing separating them. In the dim candlelight, she really looked at him and realized what was familiar about his appearance. His dark eyes, high cheekbones, full lips, chiseled jawline, and somewhat messy curls, made him a combination of two actors she thought were so gorgeous. She'd gushed over Timothée Chalamet after seeing the movie *Little Women,* and the gorgeous dark-haired Aidan Turner was from her favorite eighteenth-century series, *Poldark.* She half closed her eyes wanting so badly to touch the man sitting next to her, to hold his hand, to kiss him.

The show started with the familiar piano riff, pulling Holly from her thoughts. As the episode progressed, they laughed at the same time, and occasionally their hands touched when they reached into the bowl. After watching the first two episodes of season four, Wagner asked if she had any favorite episodes.

"Remember the 'Chair Model' episode, where Michael is trying to get everyone in the office to find him a date?" Holly asked.

"Oh, right. The one where Dwight makes everyone write down the name of someone they know and a phone number on an index card to give to Michael?"

Holly nodded then started to quote some lines. "Michael reads an index card." 'vivacious redhead.' Ring, ring." she held her hand up to her ear with her pinkie and thumb out. "Hello, Wendy? This is Michael Scott from Dunder Mifflin.' And the woman on the end of the line says, 'This is a Wendy's restaurant.'"

Holly cracked up in a way that was contagious, and Wagner started laughing too. Then Holly continued talking about the episode, laughing almost too hard to talk. She took a breath and said, "Then Dwight comes in and hands Michael a card that says 'chair model' —supposedly the model they'd thought was so hot from an office-furniture catalog. Dwight gets down on his knees and says, 'Michael this is my pledge to you. I will find her and bring her to you, and, as God is my witness, she shall bear your fruit.'"

"Oh, yeah," Wagner said. "But after Dwight calls the furniture company, who gives him the modeling agency, the agency tells him the model died in a car accident, and Michael acts like he's devastated."

Holly nods. "I know, right? And everyone in the office is looking at him like he's crazy, because he didn't even know her. Do you remember how it ends? Dwight tells him he needs closure, so they go to the cemetery and find her grave."

Wagner nodded then said, "And while standing in front of her tombstone, they start singing, like, an anthem to her to the tune of . . ." He snapped his fingers like he was trying to remember the song, then he started singing, "Bye-bye, Miss American Pie . . ."

He stood, took Holly by the hand, and tugged her up with him. Then he pulled his Spotify up on the TV and played the song by Don McLean. He turned the volume up, and together they sang along, dancing and laughing while moving to the music like they were closing down a college bar in the wee morning hours. Holly twirled into Wagner, and his hands gripped her at the waist; now they were face to face. He sang to her, and together they finished singing the song while staring into each other's eyes. For Holly it felt like the New Year's Eve scene from one of her favorite movies growing up, *High School Musical*, when Gabriella and Troy end up singing, "Start of Something New." But she couldn't mention that to Wagner, right? That would be a little too weirdish.

Suddenly, he playfully pulled her down on the couch with him and their legs were touching. Holly turned to face him. Her knee touched his thigh, and neither of them moved.

"You have a great voice, Wagner."

He gave her an enthusiastic look. "And so do you, Holly."

"I want to know more about you," Holly said. "Because I feel like I've only scratched the surface, and there is so, so much more to unpack."

He leaned in a bit closer to her, and she caught a whiff of his woodsy, tobacco scent. It made her want to run her nose along his neck up to his ear, across his jawline, and over to his mouth.

Then she realized he was talking. "Are they?" he was asking.

But Holly hadn't heard the first part of the question. "Uh, are they?" She raised her hands, palms up, and gave him a playful look.

"Tulips. Are they your favorite flower? I want to make sure I get everything right when it comes to Holly Curtis."

"Oh, yeah. I really like tulips. But if I were to pick a favorite flower, I think I would choose peonies."

"Ahh." Wagner leaned over the back of the couch until he could reach the large floral arrangement on the table behind him. He pulled out a single pink peony and handed it to Holly. "For you," he said, giving her a small bow from his seated position.

Holly ran the petals lightly across her nose, then brought the flower down to her lips. "Thank you," she whispered.

"What would you like to ask me?" Wagner asked.

Holly tilted her head to the side and considered. "What were holidays like growing up? Did your family travel to places like Aspen, Europe, or somewhere tropical during Christmas and New Year's?"

"Sometimes we did. We went to Italy one year for Christmas and went to Christmas Eve mass at the Pantheon. That was special."

"That sounds cool. Are you Catholic?"

Wagner shook his head. "No, my mother grew up Catholic, and my father is Jewish. I grew up learning about both religions. But when I got older, like around thirteen, I decided I really wanted answers, so I read the Bible—all of it, from Genesis to Revelation."

"Wow. How long did that take?"

"A little over a year. But it was so worth it. It gave me answers to things I'd wondered about. Like, I really wanted to learn more about the predictions about Jesus in the Old Testament. I wanted to better understand the scriptures that were written in those ancient times and how they would relate to me today. There are a lot of predictions and visual references—clues, so to speak, about Jesus. But by reading both the Old and New Testaments, I was able to understand much more about who God is—and why he came to earth to save people who a lot of the time seem uninterested. I learned his love for us is greater than any love we could ever know. Even though I'm not a father yet, I got the understanding that as the perfect father, he wants us to love him unconditionally, and without prodding, the same as any parent would want their child to love them."

"Oh, I've never thought of it that way," Holly said. "But I guess if you look at it from a loving-parent standpoint, the parent only wants what's best for their child. And the child isn't going to know what's best, because they only know what they want and when they want it."

Wagner nodded. "When I really began to study God's word, it became more personal to me. I realized a relationship with God is supposed to be personal. And in order to know him, we need to accept his gift of grace, and forgiveness. Apart from any form of organized beliefs or made-made religious system, it's simply between you and God. I'm still Jewish; that's part of who I am, and it always will be, but now I have a greater understanding that it's really about a personal relationship."

"So did your parents want you to be only Jewish or only Christian?"

"No. We went to temple, and I even went to Hebrew school here in the city when I was younger. And we also went to a Christian church. We celebrated both Jewish and Christian holidays. My parents were able to put aside their differences when it came to raising me and my sister. They wanted us to understand both of their faiths, so they allowed us to make the choice. And I didn't think I could decide a thing like that without actually studying the Bible. Maybe it's just me. I see things in black and white. I like to do research, and I want to know and understand things before making a leap into something that is that important. And I want to get to know you because you are very important to me too. And because you are much more than just black and white or this or that. You, Holly Curtis, color my world."

Holly dipped her head, and a shy smile graced her lips. She could feel the heat creep up her neck and into her cheeks. Wagner had really opened up to her and shared something that was not only ultimately unique about himself but also gave her a better understanding of how he thought and who he was.

"Thank you for sharing that with me, Wagner." She moved her hand to rest on top of his knee. "I know that is something really personal, and it's an important part of who you are. I can see how sharing something that personal could feel intimidating, but it means you feel that you can trust me, and that's a really good feeling. I can see how growing up practicing both Judaism and Christianity could have been something that sparked your curiosity. And I can appreciate your need to search deeper to gain understanding." Wagner placed his hand on top of Holly's, and his eyes were focused on hers as she continued. "We always just went to a non-denominational church when I was growing up," she said. Both of my parents were raised Christian. I was pretty active in Young Life in high school, which is a youth-oriented non-denominational social club. And I was involved with it a little in college too. But since I've been working, I don't go to church as often as I did when I lived at home."

When Holly finished speaking, they held each other's gaze. Holly opened her hand underneath Wagner's and laced her fingers with his. She inched toward him slowly, and he moved slowly toward her. With her other hand, she reached up and cupped his jaw, tugging him toward her. Their lips met gently, but soon passion took over, and the kiss deepened as their tongues danced, tasted, and caressed. Holly moved her hands up Wagner's chest, around his neck, and into his hair. When she moved to sit on his lap, his hands rose slowly up her back. One rested at the nape of her neck, and the other slipped down her side to grip her waist. When Holly moved her hand under Wagner's shirt, she brushed the soft skin across his rib cage.

Wagner broke their kiss and whispered, "Holly, you have no idea how long I've wanted to kiss you. And I want to keep kissing you. I want you to know how much I care about you." He kissed her nose, her lips, her forehead, and her neck just below her ear. He traced the line of her neck with his finger down to her collarbone. "I want to take things slow," he said. "I want to cherish you. I haven't felt this strongly about anyone, except maybe the first girl I ever fell for, then no one else until you. It's not that I'm afraid of loving you; I think I'm already falling in love with you. But I want to guard my heart, and most importantly, I want to guard *your* heart. I want to protect you like you're the most valuable thing I've ever known. I want to hold you in high esteem, Holly Curtis. The feelings I have now will only grow deeper. I don't want to rush you into anything you are not ready for either. Let's be honest with each other as we move forward and keep trust and communication at the forefront."

Holly didn't even realize she was crying until a tear rolled off her lips and splashed onto her hand. The words he'd said had pierced her soul. They'd awoken something she had not known existed, and it felt like pure love, the purest.

"I've never known anyone like you, Wagner Stein," she said. "But I'm really, really glad I do."

Wagner brushed a tear from Holly's cheek with his thumb, then placed a kiss where it had been. He pulled her to him and held her with both arms, placing gentle kisses on top of her head. She sank into his chest like it was a life raft, and she closed her eyes, feeling cherished.

Holly didn't know how long they'd been sitting and holding each other, and they might have nodded off, because they both jumped when they heard a phone ring. The ringing was coming from somewhere in the kitchen.

"I think that's my phone," Wagner said.

Holly moved off of him, and he stood and went to search for his phone. She heard him answer it. He walked back to the couch, finished the call, then sat down next to her again.

"That was Stella," he said. "I think she's been trying your number for a while, then decided to call me. There's something she said we needed to see."

36

Who's Famous Now?

Holly moved from the couch and reached for Wagner's hand. "I think my phone is still plugged in in the bedroom."

Hand in hand they walked down the hall and into the room where Holly was staying. She unplugged her phone from the charging cord and looked through what seemed to be hundreds of texts and Instagram notifications. When she found Stella's text messages, she read through them quickly. Apparently, photos from the greenroom had been posted on social media by both Beyond and Bradley's show. A pop-culture site had posted them as well and listed Holly's appearance on the show as one of their "hot takes." Stella had sent the link for Holly to take a look at. Holly moved to sit cross-legged on the bed, and Wagner sat next to her. She clicked on the link and held her phone out to show Wagner.

"Look," she said. "Are we having our own fifteen minutes of fame right now?"

Wagner looked at the phone screen and saw a photo of him and Holly along with a photo of them with Bradley. Holly read the article out loud.

"In a New York Minute host, Bradley Banner is shown with special guest and journalist Holly Curtis from *Beyond*

magazine along with the magazine's podcast editor, podcast host, and website manager Wagner Stein. The summer issue of *Beyond* recognizes Bradley Banner as the publication's 'Woman of the Year.' Curtis wrote the cover story on Banner and was a featured guest on Banner's show earlier today. Stein the son of former MGM executive Gregory Stein, accompanied her to the set."

Holly shrugged. "I guess this is good publicity?"

"It's not bad," Wagner agreed. "Since Stella posted the photos I'd sent her to the magazine's social media earlier today, my Instagram has blown up with at least a thousand more followers."

"Mine has too." Holly laughed "It's like we're the 'it' couple. Although they didn't really hint that we are 'together' in the article."

Wagner grinned. "Should we come out publicly?" he asked in a playful tone.

Holly leaned into his shoulder. Wagner pulled her onto his lap so her head was closer to his chest. She held up her phone and snapped a few selfies. Then she turned and kissed him on the cheek and snapped another pic.

"Which one should I post?" she asked.

Wagner pointed to the kiss photo. But before Holly could post it and tag him, he reached for her hands, and gently set her phone down. She turned to face him and intertwined her hands with his. He touched his forehead to hers and rested it there for a beat, then kissed the spot.

"Holly," he whispered. His lips lowered to hers, brushing against them with feathered softness. "Will you be my girlfriend?"

With a smile as wide as the sun, Holly nodded and said, "Yes, I will be your girlfriend, Wagner Stein."

He kissed her softly and slowly. Their chests rose and fell in perfect sync as Holly's kisses matched the desire she felt in the touch of his lips.

"I could kiss you forever," Wagner said. "I hope that dream comes true."

"I hope it does too," Holly said, "because I never want this to end."

37

Central Park in Spring

The next morning when Holly woke up, she found a note and a slightly wilted pink peony that had been partially slid underneath her door. She unfolded the note which said, *Can I take you to breakfast?*

She wrote back, *Yes, as long as you kiss me the way you did last night.* She signed it with a heart and slipped the note under Wagner's door. Before she got in the shower, she filled a glass with water and added the wilted Peony with hopes of it perking up. After throwing on jeans and a sweatshirt, she picked up her phone and crossbody bag and slipped on her tennis shoes. Then she walked down the hall to find Wagner standing in the living room wrapping up a phone call.

"Good morning," he said when he saw Holly walk into the room. He stepped in front of her and pulled her toward him, then tilted his head down, and slowly and softly kissed her lips. When they pulled apart, he said, "I was just talking to Marla. Her doctor plans to release her tomorrow morning. We might want to plan our flight home on Monday. And I was thinking of asking Michael and Marla to stay here tomorrow night. I could have the housekeeper make up the bed in the guest room for them. He leaned down and placed another kiss on her lips.

Holly let go of the grip she had on the back of Wagner's shirt. "Yeah," she agreed. "They would appreciate that, I'm sure."

"So, I have a great breakfast place in mind. It's just a few blocks from here."

"Lead the way," Holly said and took Wagner's hand in hers. "I'm hungry for Saturday- morning pancakes."

As they stepped onto the elevator, Wagner's phone rang. He listened to the caller with some intensity, not saying anything for a while. As they were walking through the lobby and out onto the sidewalk, Holly heard him say, "I think I can arrange that. I'll call you back in about an hour." He hung up, stuffed the phone into the front pocket of his khaki pants, and turned to Holly. "There's a surprise coming," he said.

"You're full of surprises," Holly replied.

"Yes, but this one is not mine. And I'm going to need your help to pull it off."

They crossed the street and continued down Second Avenue to East Seventy-First Street, making their way toward Café Luka on First Avenue. Along the way Wagner explained that Michael was planning to go to Tiffany's to purchase an engagement ring for Marla. He'd asked if Wagner and Holly could help him find a place to propose that would not involve much walking. Holly gasped, put a hand up to cover her mouth, stopped, and turned to face Wagner. "Are we the only ones who know?"

He nodded. "So far," he said. "But he has been talking with Marla's parents quite a bit these last few days, and I bet they know he's going to propose. I was thinking about having him take her up to the pool at The Fairmont. My parents' apartment building has a rooftop pool with great views of New York at night. We could line the edges of the pool with candles or tea lights and maybe rose petals that could be waiting for them when they got up there."

"That sounds perfect. So should we get that ready for them for tomorrow night?" Holly asked.

"Right. We could buy the flowers in the morning, and later tonight we can see if we can find the candles we need around the apartment. If not, we can get some in the morning. Tomorrow evening after they arrive, I could have dinner delivered for them, and then you and I could go out to eat. We could say we know that Marla needs to rest, and we want to give them some space."

Holly nodded. "That sounds like a good plan."

"Then after we eat, we'd just go to the pool deck, set everything up, and text Michael to tell him it was ready. We could hide up there, and we could film the proposal and take photos."

Holly turned giddy with excitement. "This is so great," she said.

After breakfast, Holly and Wagner walked hand in hand through Central Park then to the Metropolitan Museum of Art, where they spent the afternoon looking at beautiful sculptures and paintings while also sneaking in a few hot and heavy kisses. After wandering around the museum for several hours, they got ice cream and sat down on the Met steps. Holly leaned onto Wagner's shoulder, and between licks from her cone, she said, "This emergency trip has turned out to be so significantly amazing. I'm glad I came to my senses and broke the barriers I'd built up around you."

"The barriers? That sounds serious. I don't know— maybe even appalling. I think I should be offended right now." Wagner's wide smile let Holly know that he was only teasing.

"I'm just saying I had walls up, and I was definitely getting in my own way. But lessons have been learned. Now it seems as if everything is right in my world. I've been on a TV talk show. I've checked off my goal of writing a cover story— and I plan on writing more of those. Plus, I've found the man of my dreams." She laughed. "We've even been the subject of a "hot- takes" article. Should I be worried? I mean that the other shoe is about to drop?"

Wagner considered his answer then said, "There's no reason to worry. There might be things we have little to no control over, but what I know I can do is be thankful for each and every day that I get to look into your gorgeous blue eyes. And I can try my best to be the one who puts a smile on your face every single day—and to love you as if I'm living my last days and taking my last breath. Because living every day of my life being able to love you . . ." He took her hand and pulled her to stand with him, and as they faced each other, he finished his thought. "I do love you, Holly, with all of my heart."

He leaned down and kissed her passionately as if it might be his last kiss. It was a kiss as delicious as the mint chocolate chip ice cream they'd been eating; it was cold and sweet, and Holly felt as if the past and future didn't matter. Because all that felt real was that moment, which was holding everything in a single heartbeat. It was as if time was made of only beginnings, as if the past never existed, and Holly was his future, and he was hers.

38

Is Forever Even Long Enough?

Early on Sunday morning, Holly texted Garrison to send a driver to take her and Wagner to the hospital since Marla was being released. Wagner had asked the housekeeper to make up the guest room while they were gone. That way, both Michael and Marla could get some rest as soon as they arrived later that day.

Once they all arrived at The Fairmont, Wagner and Holly wanted to stay out of Michael and Marla's way, knowing how exhausted they both were from the ordeal that had begun on their flight from Atlanta. After making sure Marla was as comfortable as she could be, Holly and Wagner left to do some more fun sightseeing and touristy things around the city. First, Wagner took Holly to the top of the Empire State Building. Then they rode the subway to Wall Street, walked to the 9/11 memorial, and had lunch at a restaurant along the water overlooking the Statue of Liberty. Before they headed back to the apartment, they made a stop at a store to purchase the items they needed for the big surprise.

When they walked into the apartment, Marla's hair was in a towel, and she was dressed casually. Holly sat next to her on the couch and asked how she felt.

"I think I must have slept for six hours," Marla said. "Michael slept longer. He just got in the shower."

"We are going to order takeout for your dinner," Holly explained. "I want you guys to have a chance to have a nice evening together after what you've just been through. What do you feel like eating?"

"I'm not up for eating a big meal yet. Egg drop soup would be great. And if you do order Chinese, Michael will probably want egg rolls and kung pao chicken. But don't go to any trouble for us. We are just so thankful to you and Wagner for all you've done already."

"Well, Wagner and I are treating you guys to a special, private dinner for two tonight. So if you want Chinese, we will order that."

Marla put her hand on Holly's arm. "Holly, please don't go to any trouble for us, really. We are just glad to be out of the hospital and to be flying home tomorrow."

"Nope, Marla. This time you are taking it easy, and we are doing everything for you. I also suggest that you put on something nice and a bit less casual. Trust me on that. You guys have been stuck in a hospital since you arrived in New York. Tonight is going to be a special date night, just the two of you."

Holly winked at her, but Marla just seemed confused. Her look was like, *What the heck? I just got home from the hospital, and dressing up was so not on the agenda for tonight.*

Holly kept nodding, as if that might convince Marla to change clothes. Then she said, "Trust me. You'll want to change."

Marla still looked a bit perplexed but eventually agreed, and with a smile she said, "Okay. I appreciate you trying to make our last night here so special, Holly. It's so very much like you to be so thoughtful, always looking out for me."

A few hours later, Holly placed the order for the food to be delivered. After she hung up, she and Wagner set the table in the kitchen for a romantic dinner for two. They added candles and the vase of tulips from Friday night. Then he got out two glasses and a bottle of wine and set those on the table too. As soon as the food arrived, they would plate it, light the candles, call for Marla and Michael, then sneak out the door.

* * * * * *

Wagner had made a dinner reservation for him and Holly at a cozy, intimate candlelit Italian restaurant within walking distance from The Fairmont. Holly brought her large tote, which was filled with tea lights, a lighter, and a bouquet of red roses to use for creating a pathway of petals. When they were almost finished with dinner, Wagner sent a quick text to Michael to let him know they were about to go set everything up. Holly was beside herself with excitement. Honestly, she was just so happy that she could do something for Marla.

When Wagner and Holly got to the roof, Holly dropped rose petals as she walked toward the pool. Wagner lined part of the edge of the pool with candles, and Holly sprinkled more rose petals near those. Then she pulled up a small table and set a single long-stemmed rose on it. Wagner lit all the candles, then texted Michael. Then he and Holly moved behind a cluster of potted trees and waited.

About fifteen minutes later, they could hear Marla and Michael making their way from the elevator toward the pool. Michael was making comments about the view. As they approached the pool, Marla noticed the pathway of petals. "Someone must be planning a party, Michael," she said. "Maybe we shouldn't be up here."

"Let me just show you something," he coaxed her. "Just a little further."

When they'd made it to the section of the pool deck where the view of the New York skyline was the best, Michael dropped down to one knee. Holly and Wagner pulled their phones out. Wagner made a video while Holly snapped photos. Marla's face was filled with shock and elation as she started to realize what was happening. Michael opened a box with a sparkling diamond from Tiffany's inside and held it out to Marla. Marla's hands went to her face, and happy tears began to fall.

"Marla Monique Monroe, you are the best thing that has ever happened to me. And I don't want to say I was scared into proposing tonight, but I could say I needed a push, something to make me see how important every day is. A reminder not to waste a moment and to celebrate every tiny second. I want to celebrate every day with you. Will you be my wife?"

They were both crying by this time. Marla said yes, and Michael placed the ring on her finger, then handed her the long-stemmed rose. That was when Wagner and Holly walked out from behind the plants and ran over to congratulate their boss and their friend. Several photos were taken of the happy couple with the New York Skyline in the background. Wagner and Holly also took a few staged photos of the ring, and the flower petals—and even one of Michael scooping Marla up into his arms. It was a lovely ending to their New York trip after a somewhat nightmarish beginning.

After the photo session wrapped up and the candles were blown out, Marla leaned in close to Holly's ear and said, "I am so glad you finally said yes to Wagner. Because if you hadn't come around, it might have broken my heart as much as it would have broken his. I know he's liked you for a while, and I started to notice the two of you getting more friendly right before this trip. And to see you two together, holding hands, warms my heart. He's a keeper."

"You're right, Marla," Holly agreed. "I'm glad I came to my senses and saw what was right in front of me. I guess sometimes a trip to New York City is all you need."

Marla smiled, and with a slight shake of her head asked, "Can you tell me when it was that you decided to give him a chance?"

Holly thought for a moment, then said, "At the tulip tea, I had an honest conversation with someone about certain things and how those things ought to be. And I think tulips are beautiful, but they're just not the flowers for me. And most definitely, this quick trip to the city might have been when Wagner came into the spotlight and showed me what my future could be. It was here that my past was revisited and the present became certain—with Wagner in my future. He's stolen my heart, and I'm happily throwing away the key."

Epilogue

A lot can happen in twenty-four hours, and sometimes bad things can turn into great things. Even after the Beyond crew got back together in the Atlanta office, things continued to go well. Marla worked from home the first week back while still recuperating, and that gave her time to plan her wedding, and book the location. She chose the Jekyll Island Club Resort, a beautiful and historic property located on a small barrier island off the coast of Georgia. She selected the first Saturday in November, simply because it would give her a few months to get the final wedding details in order once the fall issue was released in September.

And, yes, in case you are wondering, Michelle Obama was on the cover of that fall issue. And *Beyond's* reputation and exposure have continued to grow. Now, a full year later, the staff has just released another summer issue and opened an office in Orange County, California. Marla and Michael moved there to run that office and decided to start a family. Marla's family is from the area, and they are glad to have them close to home, especially with the first granddaughter on the way. There is talk about the possibility of Beyond expanding into Europe, and a publishing house in Paris has been knocking on the door. Who would be perfect to run an office for Beyond in Paris? You might have some ideas.

When Marla moved to California, Holly was put in charge of the Atlanta office. Stella is now in charge of marketing and advertising accounts. Joe still handles design, graphics, and production. Wagner is busy handling both the Atlanta and California websites and is still the podcast editor and host, occasionally traveling to California to interview guests. Kali still works in photography, but now she has a crew of photographers and social media people she manages.

Holly's roommate, Lofton met a law student from Emory. He is Holly-approved, he's definitely a cat person, and all is going well for them. Denim finished her London theater internship, then stayed a few months longer before returning home in November. In December she got to walk in UGA's graduation. She's now in New York auditioning to be in Broadway productions. Holly still keeps in touch with the girls she met at the Tulip Tea. She's even thinking about planning another trip to the beach house in Montauk. And Lydia is now a big fan of Holly, crediting her story in *Beyond* for pushing Bradley Banner into a victory in the governor's race. Lydia might have even casually mentioned to Holly a few times that she wanted to leave her the Montauk house in her will.

What hasn't changed in the past year? Trivia Tuesdays. And with the summer issue in the books, and with a Tuesday workday behind them, the crew is heading out to play against their nemesis, Bane of Your Existence. Some of the younger members of the office crew have started playing trivia too and have even started their own team, but they have yet to come close to getting in the top three. Not much has changed with Trivia Tuesdays, except that Holly now rides to trivia with Wagner. The Beyond Amazing team has also had to train a new waitress to be their favorite since Darby recently graduated from Georgia State and moved to Dallas.

"Remember, Courtney, that Joe and Kali like slices of lime on their glasses," Stella instructed their new, not quite favorite waitress. "Wagner prefers an orange slice but will tolerate a lime, and Holly and I always get top-shelf margaritas on the rocks with sugar, not salt."

"Don't be so hard on her," Holly said, slapping at Stella's arm. "Courtney, don't mind Stella."

Before Courtney walked away, Stella gave her a thumbs-up, maybe to soften the edge.

"Are you wanting her to hate us and loathe seeing us walk through the doors every Tuesday night or what?" Kali asked.

Stella shushed Kali because Trivia Guy was giving the categories. "Did you hear what he said?" Stella asked.

"I wrote them down. We have current events, geography, British literature, pop culture, and science," Kali said.

"Science!" Wagner and Joe said in loud, deep voices.

As the first round progressed, they were feeling pretty good about their score. When the answers to the bonus question had been turned in for round one, Trivia Guy called for a representative from team Beyond Amazing to come up to his booth. Over the loudspeaker he explained that there was an apparent discrepancy with their answer.

"Joe, what did you write down?" Stella asked.

Joe shrugged. "You guys were naming off all the top movies you thought were box-office hits between 2005 and 2010, and I only wrote the ones you said."

"Okay," Stella said. "Will you go see what he wants?"

"Wait, Joe," Wagner said. "Let's send Holly. Holly, will you go see what he wants, please?"

"Sure," Holly said.

She got up from the table and walked over to the trivia guy. When she got there, he looked up at her, and with microphone in hand said, "There's a question that needs answering."

Holly nodded and waited for him to ask it. The trivia guy paused a beat then said, "In order for you to answer this question, I need you to turn around, and face the audience."

Holly shrugged and gave the trivia guy a questioning look but then turned around. There in front of her, Wagner was down on one knee. A small box was popped open in his hand, displaying a sparkling engagement ring, and he looked up at her and said, "Holly Elaine Curtis, from the first moment I saw you, I knew I wanted to know everything about you. Then one year ago, I had the opportunity to spend a whole weekend with you. I could say that was the best weekend of my life, but then there was the next weekend and the next with you by my side, and they just kept getting better and better. Some might say good things don't last forever, but they've never met Holly Curtis, or fallen in love with her. Without you, Holly, my world would lack color and fun, and you know this already, but you color my world. And every day with you is like finding gold at the end of a rainbow. Holly, will you marry me?"

Holly screamed, "Yes! A million, trillion times yes. I was wondering what was taking you so long to ask!"

Wagner stood, placed the ring on Holly's finger, pulled her close to him, and said, "First, I wanted to make sure I could ride to trivia with you."

Holly giggled at his answer. Then he kissed her deeply in front of a room filled with restaurant patrons who were all standing and cheering so loudly that no one could possibly hear what the next question or set of categories would be. Once trivia was over, the first person Holly called to share the good news with was her mom.

Author's Note

This is my sixth romance novel, and on a whim, I decided to try my hand at writing a romantic comedy. I certainly hope I gave you a few laughs. This wasn't the story I originally planned to write. After writing my last book, a historical romance, I thought I'd write a contemporary romance with elements of history mixed in. But that book was going to require a great deal of research, which at the time I just could not fit into my schedule. So after taking a quick trip to New York City with my daughter on May 19, 2023, where I was to give an award to a historian that I'd met while doing research for my historical fiction. We attended a Tulip Tea benefit, and it gave me the idea for this story. Honestly, I had planned for the old high school crush to be the "one," like, part of a rekindled romance so to speak. But for some reason, the character of Wagner Stein called to me more, and it became clearer as I continued to write that he was really the "one."

I wanted the story to not only be lighthearted, and fun, but to also feel real and warm. I wanted to explore what it might be really like when two people who seem to be an unlikely match find common ground through mutual trust and understanding, through being open and honest, real, and respectful toward one another. And I really wanted to show what the "perfect guy" might look like if such a thing exists, and we can always hold out hope for that!

Some might have disliked the part where Wagner explains what it was like for him to grow up with both Jewish and Christian parents who taught their children the traditions of both religions, allowing each to choose which one they preferred or maybe felt more of a calling toward. I wanted that scene to feel like an intimate, heartfelt moment that was real and raw. I wanted it to also touch the hearts of those who might have needed to read that passage. I never know who will find my books or read them, and I hope somewhere I've touched someone's heart or soul with a profound realness that speaks directly to them, even if they are the only person that passage speaks to. I know that might seem super cheesy and a little weird, but it's something I feel strongly about.

And I want my mostly female audience to know and understand how important it is to stand up for what you know is right, speak your mind and be appreciated for what you have to say. Know that as a woman, you deserve to be heard, to be treated with the upmost respect. And when you find the "one" you will know him by the way he loves you, respects you and holds you in high esteem. He will put you first and will treasure your heart as the most precious thing in the world. He most definitely will not take advantage of you, or use you, and he will wait patiently because you are worth waiting for.

I hope you enjoyed *The Tulip Tea: Twenty-Four Hours in NYC*. If so, please leave a review on Amazon or Goodreads, post and tag me on social media, or invite me to speak at one of your book-club events. You can connect with me in the following ways. Email: perrietuck@mac.com, website: www.perriepatterson.com My Instagram accounts are: @always.n.style or @thetalkingbookatlanta, Facebook: Perrie Patterson Author or The Talking Book Podcast and TikTok: @authorperriepatterson. Retailers can purchase my books through ingramspark.com.

Special Thank You's

Having great beta readers who give honest feedback about the first drafts of my novels is priceless. I cannot give them enough praise and thank-yous. I take their opinions into consideration as I add clarification to some passages and even make deletions. Their comments always help to make a book just a little better than what I'd first put down on the pages. Thank you, betas, for reading horrible rough drafts. Your time and effort mean the world. Thank you to author Julane Fisher, author Josie Kerr, my book-club buddy, Paula Butler. Thanks as well to Tali Mullins, my cousin by marriage, who is an avid reader, and to my mother-in-law, Eileen Tucker who is a former teacher.

And, finally, I have one of the best editors ever! Huge thanks always go out to my editor, Mary Beth Bishop. Thank you. My proofreader for this book was Andie Martin. Thank you all so very much. And thank you to everyone who read this, and took a chance on an unknown author, it means the world.

Discussion Questions for Groups

1. This book is the author's first try at writing comedy. Did you find some parts to be funny? If so, name one or two.
2. What did you like about the characters? Did you have a favorite character or one that you related to more than the others?
3. Did you feel a bit sorry for Wagner Stein early on in the story?
4. Did you think Holly was going to fall head-over-heels in love with her old high school flame? What was your reaction to his forwardness/assault? Did you agree or disagree with the way Holly handled that situation? How would you handle a situation like that, or what advice would you give to someone who might have gone through something very similar? Have you tried to prepare someone for a situation like that so they would know what to do if something similar occurred?
5. At what point did you start pulling for Holly to get together with Wagner?
6. Were you disappointed that this story left out steamy scenes? Or did you enjoy the more innocent, sweeter nature of this romance?
7. Talk a little about the feminist aspect of the story. Was it something that was a plus for this book?
8. Talk about the concept of *Beyond* magazine and the fact that it features only women, spotlighting subjects from all walks of life from around the world who share their unique and interesting stories. Did you find this to be a cool concept?
9. What was something you would have liked to have seen more of in the story?
10. Would you recommend this book as a quick "beach read" to a friend?

More Books by Perrie Patterson

The *Crimson* Trilogy
New adult romances set on the University of Alabama campus.
Walking the Crimson Road
My Blood Runs Crimson
All the Crimson Roses
The last two books in the series are best suited for readers who are eighteen and older.

Hit Zero
Young-adult sports romance set against the background of competition cheerleading.

Leader of Liberty: Tale of America's First Spy Ring
Historical-fiction romance set during the American Revolution.

Each of my books has its own Spotify playlist. You can find the playlist for *The Tulip Tea* by searching "Perrie Tucker" and the Playlist title "Ticket to the Tulip Tea" on Spotify. And here is the song list you will see:

"Picture to Burn" by Taylor Swift
"American Pie" by Don McLean
"Start of Something New" from Disney's High School Musical
"Breakfast at Tiffany's" the original 1950s version by Henry Mancini
"Blank Space" by Taylor Swift
"Breakfast at Tiffany's" by Deep Blue Something
"We are Never Ever Getting Back Together" by Taylor Swift
"Getaway Car" by Taylor Swift
"New York, New York" by Frank Sinatra
"Ready for It" by Taylor Swift
"No Body No Crime" by Taylor Swift, featuring HAIM
"I Did Something Bad" by Taylor Swift
"The Office Theme Song" by the Mount Royal Orchestra
"Blank Space" by Taylor Swift
"The Man" by Taylor Sift
"Our Song" by Taylor Swift
"Love Song" by Taylor Sift
"You Belong with Me" by Taylor Swift

About the Author

Perrie is a graduate of the University of Alabama, who had no idea that her fashion- merchandising degree would lead her to write romance novels. Now that both her children are older—one is a college graduate and the other is going to graduate from UGA in the spring, Perrie and her husband, Jeff, have more time for traveling to research Perrie's novels. When not writing, Perrie volunteers in multiple roles. She is a mentor for the Forsyth County School System and a member of the Chestatee River NSDAR, in which she holds three positions. Perrie leads a ladies' Bible study through Brown's Bridge Community Church. Through that group, she is helping put together an annual fundraiser for the local Cumming, Georgia, nonprofit Jesse's House (www.jesseshouse.org) Since 1998, Jesse's House has helped more than 1,092 girls throughout the state of Georgia receive care and protection from unsafe living conditions, neglect, and human trafficking. Jesse's House provides a safe undisclosed location where the girls get their own rooms, along with medical, and dental care and therapy while they finish high school. Perrie is also a member of the Forsyth County Optimists Club.

Perrie is also a facilitator for her neighborhood book club. And she interviews authors on a podcast called, *The Talking Book Atlanta*. You can find *The Talking Book Atlanta* on Facebook, Instagram, and Spotify.

Perrie loves opportunities to speak to groups and book clubs. Please feel free to email her at perrictuck@mac.com or reach out through her website: www.perriepatterson.com or Instagram: @always.n.style.

www.ingramcontent.com/pod-product-compliance
Lightning Source LLC
LaVergne TN
LVHW041756060526
838201LV00046B/1027